DISCIPLESHIP IS LEADERSHIP

Stages of Generational Development

BY RICH GRIFFITH

Discipleship Is Leadership: Stages of Generational Development

Published by D6 Family Ministry
114 Bush Road
Nashville, TN 37217
Visit d6family.com

ISBN: 9781614841869

Printed in the United States of America

Acknowledgements

I thank the following individuals and organizations for making this work possible.

For the leadership of D6 Family Ministry who believed in my work and have helped me sharpen my theological thinking.

For the leadership of Toccoa Falls College that has allowed me to take that thinking and apply it to both academic and practitioner settings. After completing a doctorate in youth, family, and culture, I was able to complete a master's degree in organizational leadership. It has refined my thinking and application of leadership and discipleship practices.

Finally, I thank two of our undergraduate students, Hannah McLaughlin and Kamryn Ruh, who took the time to read over the manuscript of this book and make helpful editing suggestions.

Table of Contents

Creating Years – "I Have Purpose in God"

Introduction

An accepted definition of discipleship is "the process by which the Holy Spirit works through the inspired Word, related materials, and Spirit-empowered workers to 1) lead individuals to Christ, 2) build them up in Christ, and 3) equip them for effective, lifelong ministry for Christ"[1] (Parker, 1999, 19). Before the term "discipleship" had become in vogue, there was "Christian education" with its emphasis on "Christian nurture." If these are acceptable definitions, we are forced to ask several questions. For instance, why is America becoming increasingly secularized if churches are doing an excellent job of discipleship? Why has the evangelical church been retaining only 25% of youth who grew up in youth ministries, and why are those youth not involved in effective lifelong ministry as adults? Have we relied on the Holy Spirit? Are we leading others to Christ and building them up in Christ, or have we been too busy building church buildings and programs? Ultimately, the question we have to ask is, Have we as parents been effective in helping our children follow Christ into adulthood?

In writing this book, I envisioned two parents walking hand-in-hand with their child. Why do we hold our child's hand? On the one hand (no pun intended), it is a sign of our affection for our child. On the other hand, it is a gesture of protecting our child. Holding our child's hand says, "I love you. We belong to each other, and I am here to protect and lead you." Think about a time when you grabbed your child's hand as you walked along in a parking lot or crossed the street. Reaching out and taking your child's hand is instinctual. Then I thought about this image metaphorically. It seems that we as parents in our society have stopped "holding our children's hands." Maybe we have become too overwhelmed with the various things our children are exposed to.

After finishing my doctorate and while serving as a professor at Toccoa Falls College, I have continued to minister to families in a local church setting. I continue to research and engage in youth culture. After my doctorate, however, I completed a second master's degree in organizational leadership. With years of ministry and education experience, along with being a dad, I believe the Lord has laid it upon my heart to write more about discipleship, leadership, and culture. We have made discipleship too difficult by professionalizing it. As many of us work, we live in a culture that seems fixated with leadership. We seem to keep leadership compartmentalized to our work and service to other organizations, but we may not be so cognizant or intentional about our leadership in our homes. However, as the title of this book declares, Discipleship *IS* Leadership!

I want to go back to my illustration about handholding for just a moment. I write this as a single dad of three sons. When we take our children's hands to walk with them, to offer them security, to show affection, and to guide them, our children feel a sense of belonging and safety. A child is even more secure when two parents are holding that child's hands. In previous writings I have also explained that I have intentionally put godly women into the lives of my sons because young men need to understand life from a woman's perspective. Metaphorically, once again, we are letting go of our children's hands at younger and younger ages, and, further, there are fewer hands in their lives to hold. If I can be frank, single parenthood is not the ideal. I understand "things" happen, and I am in no way bashing single parents. I ***am*** saying that no matter what type of parent and home structure a child lives with, a child needs multiple hands to hold in order to successfully navigate through life.

I also understand that parents stop holding their children's hands (in real life) when their children get older. It is unlikely that my 15-year-old son will want to hold my hand when walking out in public. (It should be stated, however, that no longer showing family cohesiveness through familial affection is very much a culturally indoctrinated way of thinking. Our lack of affection has been a product of American "rugged, manly, Western individualism.") While my 15-year-old and I do not hold hands in public, my son is still affectionate at home. I love that he still wants hugs. I love that we frequently say, "I love you." So, while we are not literal handholding in public, I am still giving emotional support to my children. In fact, as both parents and children mature, it is not uncommon for healthy parent/child relationships to express hugging. Further, discipleship is not only leadership but also nurture! One final usage of the metaphor, if I may. If we stop holding the hands of our children, there are many more nefarious entities out there willing to grasp on to our children's hands. If you read *Voices: Helping Our Children and Youth Listen to Wise Counsel,* you will begin to understand who those negative voices are. Even then, I could not encapsulate all the nefarious entities without writing a lengthy book similar to Tolstoy's *War and Peace.*

This book has a consistent layout throughout. I will begin each chapter by discussing the innovator or developer of a particular leadership model such as "Servant Leader," and a description of that leadership model will follow. I will then lay out the psychosocial developmental stage as described by famed child psychologist Erik Erikson (1950).[2]

It should be noted that, for the sake of discipleship, I may not follow the age parameters Erikson describes. In fact, even Erikson's stages are not cemented in *exact* ages, since children develop at different rates. That the stages are not an exact science is especially true of children in the context of discipleship. Next, I will show how the psychosocial and the leadership models overlap. Life stories and practical experiences will be given to discuss how discipleship practices can be engaged. Finally, I will finish with a biblical example of a person who displayed that leadership characteristic. I am not saying that each leadership model is the 100% absolute model; however, I believe it offers us a road map in thinking about a better way to disciple and lead our children.

My ultimate goal is to "simplify" discipleship so we as parents, grandparents, youth workers, teachers, and anyone else who cares about our children and youth can confidently engage in discipleship as leadership. Of all the things I have done with my life, being a parent and a leader in my family has been the most important. Don't misunderstand me; I still make mistakes and certainly wish I could have done things differently when my kids were growing up. However, with learning comes maturity and *vice versa*. People who stop learning also stop growing and maturing. We become our own echo chamber. Honestly, I wish I knew then what I know now. Here is the good news, however; no matter how much you "blew it," there are hundreds of thousands of parents who probably feel the same way. In reality, our children will respect us even more if we model a willingness to apologize for our mistakes, try to make them right, learn from them, and then improve. We are all works in progress! Maturing and growing in the grace and likeness of Jesus Christ is part of our sanctification process. Every day we strive to look more like Jesus! The process of sanctification takes humility, discipleship, and leadership. It is my hope that we will continue to pray for each other and journey with each other as we look to disciple and lead our children! Amen!

One final note: every individual in leadership has a certain style of leadership they tend to rely on. I am not stating that, as parents, we need to master every leadership style. What I am advocating for is to make ourselves more aware of the various leadership models available to us and then to practice them. Further, Christian nurture and discipleship are the very reasons we need to build a community of support around our families and our children. I strongly advocate for mentoring our children, and the younger mentoring can start, the better for our children. As an adult, I still need mentoring. If I am weak in a particular model of leadership that my child needs, I can hopefully rely on someone in my support group to provide the type of mentoring my child needs during certain phases of his life. Take heart. Growing in leadership skills is like the life-long process of sanctification. We fail only if we stop trying.

Questions

1. Why is it important to understand the developmental needs of our children when it comes to discipleship?

2. Have you ever considered applying leadership models to discipleship?

3. What are you most excited about learning when it comes to discipleship? What are your concerns or fears?

4. While you may not be familiar with the leadership models we are about to engage in, are there any leadership models you might consider one of your strengths? A weakness?

Core Years

"I Am Loved by God"

(Birth–3 Years)

Chapter 1

Leadership Model: Christ

Leadership Theory

Servant Leadership for Discipleship (Ages Birth–1.5)

Erikson's Stage

Trust Versus Mistrust — Biblical Examples: Jesus and Paul

The main theorist of servant leadership is Robert K. Greenleaf,[3] along with his protege, Larry Spears. Greenleaf wrote *Servant Leadership: A Journey into the Nature of Legitimate Power and Greatness* (1977). What makes servant leadership appealing in ministry and family contexts is that it is unique since it puts the follower's needs first. Servant leadership has ten characteristics of a servant leader: listening, empathy, healing, awareness, persuasion, conceptualization, foresight, stewardship, commitment to growth of people, and building community. Servant leaders also tend to be highly ethical as they look to develop and nurture their followers, often displaying a responsibility to those who are less fortunate.

Here we have an opportunity to mention that there is a difference between servant leadership as put forth in a secular sense and biblical servant leadership. Biblical servant leadership, as put forth by Howell (2003)[4] and Wilkes (1998)[5] makes the distinction that biblical servant leadership is defined by proven godly character displayed by the leader. Further, biblical servant leaders are driven by doxological and kingdom-driven motives. A doxological motive is a way of thinking about life and mission that focuses on the glory of God. A kingdom-driven motive is that in which a leader labors to see God's kingdom break forth on earth through their work.

One potential weakness is that researchers are not able to find consensus on a common definition or theoretical framework for servant leadership. Further, there is no clarity on whether conceptualizing, which is one of the traits of servant leadership, is a behavioral or cognitive ability. Servant leadership may very well be both. In other words, servant leadership can be seen by the outward actions of the leader who has internal motivations to function as a servant leader.

Another potential weakness is that not everyone benefits from servant leadership. If you continue to interact with a follower through servant leadership, there may be resentment on the part of the follower because they might think or feel that you do not trust them to complete tasks. As children get older, they need you to "let go" and allow them to pursue some of their own abilities. A failure to do so, even if well-intentioned, can lead to a sense of codependency.

According to Erik Erikson's first psychosocial developmental stage, a person must address the conflict of trust versus mistrust to help a child develop attachment to caregivers. It is not a coincidence that trust is a primary element of most leadership theories. In fact, due to the nature of servant leadership as described above shares common characteristics of being a servant leader in the home. As a parent and one who provides Christian nurture for your children, it is no wonder that trust is the foundation of both psychosocial development and many leadership theories—especially servant leadership.

It is not simply enough to have a child's basic needs met. Trust is developed when a child is fed, cleaned, has her diaper changed, and more, as psychological bonds of trust are strengthened during these earliest stages of life. When a child is breastfed, there is significant bonding going on between the mother and child. A child learns by the facial expressions and the voice of the mother. These are God-given ways of forming both physical and emotional attachments. When a child is comforted while also having basic needs met, these attachments are deepened, and trust is built. The opposite is also true. When a child is not nurtured while having basic needs met, the child develops a personality that lacks trust.

If we recall the characteristics of servant leadership, it is no wonder it fits most with Erikson's first stage of trust versus mistrust. A child picks up social cues when he listens to the parent sing lullabies or speak warmly to the child. Further, it has been shown that a mother can easily pick out the cry of her child even in the midst of a number of other children. When children are very small, emotionally healthy parents are in tune with the noises their child makes. Parents are often able to determine the child's need by the child's cries. It is only when a child displays an unusual behavior out of the ordinary that a parent is unable to understand the cry of her child. When it comes to building empathy, healthy parents relate to the needs of their children because they understand the need for community in addition to meeting basic needs. It is an empathetic heart that drives parents to be the best parents they can be. When it comes to healing, nurturing parents are distressed when something is wrong with their child but the issue is not obvious. Parents make every attempt to keep their child healthy.

Both healthy parents and healthy leaders have a keen awareness of what is going on in the lives of those around them. Healthy parents are ever vigilant to meet the needs of their newborn and toddler. In fact, it is this awareness that allows a child to thrive because the parent (and leader) is making sure they are perceptive to needs even before they happen. For instance, as a toddler is moving toward a hot stove, or any other item that might be considered dangerous, the parent will persuade the child to avoid the bad decision because the parent can conceptualize the negative results the child cannot.

When it comes to meeting the needs of our children, there are a couple of ways attentive parents practice foresight. All parents must have the foresight to prepare a bottle, preventatively check a diaper, and plan to purchase needs for the baby. These are the practical foresights. However, how many parents have dreams for their children and desire to put proper steps in place so their child can thrive? When it comes to stewardship, the cost of having a baby is significant. Stewarding finances to put the needs of a child first is critical. However, stewardship does not end there—especially when it comes to discipling a child. As a newborn becomes a toddler, Christian parents desire to steward the personality and future that is developing for the child and within the child.

Mary experienced stewarding the life of Jesus in the early years of His childhood. Luke 2:19 informs us, "Mary treasured up all these things and pondered them in her heart." Clearly, an attentive parent is also committed to the growth of the child while building the first community the child will be exposed to—the family. It is not a stretch to see that all these characteristics of servant leadership are essential for a child's healthy development.

Once again, servant leadership fits family life well because it has characteristics where the leader (that's you) puts the follower's (that's your child) needs first. Further, servant leaders are highly ethical and have a priority to nurture the follower before meeting their own needs. Countless good parents have sacrificed so much energy, time, money, and their own personal desires to meet the needs of their children, often before meeting their own needs. If parents are displaying all the attributes of servant leadership, children can build trust first in the home and then in the community. In particular, Spears identifies ten servant leadership characteristics:[6]

- Listening—a commitment to listening intently to others, coupled with periods of reflection.
- Empathy—an effort to understand, empathize with, and accept others.
- Healing—a focus on helping others overcome emotional wounds and aid in a search for wholeness.
- Awareness—general awareness and self-awareness, which contribute to an understanding of issues related to power, ethics, and values.

- Persuasion—in contrast to authoritarian leadership, a reliance on convincing others based on the merit of arguments rather than on coercion or manipulation.
- Conceptualization—an ability to think beyond day-to-day realities and dream big.
- Foresight—efforts to "understand lessons from the past, the realities of the present, and the likely consequence of a decision for the future."
- Stewardship—behaving with the understanding that one has been entrusted with running the organization for the greater good of society.
- Commitment to the growth of people holds the belief "that people have an intrinsic value beyond their intangible contributions as workers" leads to a strong commitment to the individual within an organization.
- Building community—a desire to create true community within the organization and other institutions.

All three of my sons were adopted. From varying degrees of least traumatic to most traumatic, all my sons missed the nurturing that was so essential to their development. They missed significant nurturing because their parents were involved in addictive drug behaviors. My sons rarely, if ever, had their birthdays, milestones, or holidays celebrated. It is obvious that my sons experienced significant neglect, while one of my sons also experienced significant abuse. You can imagine how these set up significant distrust issues in my sons. The good news is while not all "nature" issues (e.g., genetics) can be overcome by nurture, neuroscience has shown that nurture can overcome many of the developmental deficits children experience due to neglect and abuse. What is fascinating about the fact that nurture can help overcome trauma from a highly dysfunctional past is that the Bible makes the claim of healthy nurturing well before science was aware of the concept of neuroplasticity. Not until recent times has the science of neuroplasticity come to light. Brain scans and other evidence have shown that new neuropathways can be developed within the brain. Of course, Scripture has already told us that a mind can be changed in Romans 12:2, "Do not conform to the pattern of this world, but be transformed by the renewing of your mind."

As parents we always wonder if we made mistakes and if it is too late to correct those mistakes. We have just seen that, by God's grace and design, it is never too late to move toward redemption and healing. Further, there are therapies and practices that can help your child overcome deficiencies from previous years. Whether you are a parent who wants to better nurture your child or if you are an adoptive parent helping your child overcome years of trauma, it is never too late to start taking steps in a more positive direction. Children who have come from homes with drug addiction and other issues missed some of the nurture that comes naturally through breastfeeding. There are practices that can simulate the nurturing they missed.

One of my children who experienced significant abuse and trauma, participated in attachment therapy with me. For example, the way to simulate the nurture needed during infancy and bonding through breast feeding is to have the child lay comfortably across your lap while cradling his head. This allows the child and the parent to look into each other's eyes and see each other's facial expressions. As part of one of my son's therapeutic practices, we engaged in this activity through the guidance of an attachment therapist. I have to admit, as an Army veteran, holder of a black belt in tae kwon do, and someone who is not the most nurturing person, this activity was initially a bit awkward for me and my son. My son and I tried to make this attachment exercise as emotionally comfortable as possible. The therapist's instructions were to simply have a conversation that started out with easy questions. After an easy question or two, I would feed my child some chocolate or a food he really enjoyed. After the initial awkwardness subsided, we were able to engage in deeper conversations. As we engaged in further conversations, the awkwardness faded, and we began a bonding process. My son was around 11 when we did these exercises. I have been told that these approaches also work for adults who engage in these types of therapies. The approach I just described was just one way of engaging in attachment therapy. The difference my church community and I saw was nothing short of miraculous. John Bowlby was the primary theorist on attachment therapy. I have included a link to a *Psychology Today* article in the Endnotes that can help you understand attachment-based therapy.[7]

The reason I am describing this awkward, but much needed, attachment therapy experience is because servant leadership can, at times, feel very awkward. As awkward as the attachment therapy exercise I described felt for me initially, engaging in the practice was not about me meeting a need I had, it was about meeting a need my son had. As parents, we are always pushed beyond our comfort zones. We will make sacrifices and experience humility in a way we never pictured when we were younger and immature. How many dads have let their daughters braid their hair, apply nail polish, or do something that was out of character for dads? How many moms have nurtured their child in ways that came with great sacrifice beyond what is "convenient"?

When our children trust us because we have nurtured them while sacrificing our own desires, they more readily accept being discipled. Our nurturing and sacrifices show the heart of God who also nurtures and sacrifices for us. As parents, grandparents, or caregivers, we are the *imago Dei*—the image bearers of God. If we do not nurture or are aloof, our children will have a distorted image of God, as they will see God as distant and uncaring. Not until I became a parent did I begin to understand the deeper meaning of God's calling us His "adopted children" (Luke 20:34–36; Romans 8:14–17; 1 John 3:1). Further, I did not understand the process of sanctification until I became a parent. Adopting children certainly forced me to become less ego-centric and to put the desires of my children over my own desires. In fact, the more mature I became as a parent, the more I had to surrender the thought that my children reflect me. When I recognize my children reflect me, I forget that they too are the *imago Dei*. My children are created in the image of God, and I would much rather my children be more like Christ than like me! To help my children look more like Jesus and less like me, I have to model trusting God more than I trust myself. Further, I had to allow my children to experience more "natural consequences," to their actions (within reason). If I did not have a change in my thinking in these areas of my life, I would have gone against Paul's advice to not provoke my children. Ephesians 6:4 is a specific verse that speaks to discipleship: "Fathers, do not exasperate your children; instead, bring them up in the training and instruction of the Lord."

Each of my sons is different from each other. As much as I may have wanted my sons to practice martial arts or play soccer, it would have been damaging for me to impose my desires and image upon them. How many times have you seen parents go overboard at a sporting event because they lived vicariously through their children? How many parents have seen their children's choices be "direct reflections" on themselves? Do we want our children to look more like us or more like God? We are not off the hook when it comes to discipling our children. In fact, we are clearly called to instruct and discipline our children, but the underlying principle for discipleship is to let our children become who God created them to be, not who we want them to be.

Biblical Examples of Servant Leadership

Jesus Serving the World

The most obvious example of servant leadership is, of course, Jesus. Jesus displayed great servant leadership by washing the feet of the disciples (John 13:1–17). While washing His disciples' feet was one significant incident, Jesus displayed many acts of servant leadership. We often think about Jesus' sacrifice on the cross, and, yes, giving His life is the most sacrificial act. However, we must also remember that Jesus left perfect paradise to put on the flesh of humanity. While fully God, being willing to take on human flesh shows us that Jesus had incredible empathy with our suffering (Isaiah 53:3) and temptation (Matthew 4). Taking on human flesh allowed the God of the Universe to be crucified. It will be highly unlikely that most of us will face a literal crucifixion upon a cross, but we are called to crucify our pride and unbiblical ambitions. The practice of feet washing is an incredible act of humility that allows us to engage in the process of mortification, the process of learning to die to ourselves. Washing the feet of weary travelers was often the task of the lowliest servant (Watt, 2017).[8] Imagine just how nasty the feet of travelers were on the dusty roads around Jerusalem! Truth be told, if we have changed countless diapers, washing the feet of someone is not nearly as gag inducing! At one point early in my military service, I had to learn how to change diapers on about 20 pre-potty-trained babies and toddlers because the childcare workers did not show up for a watchnight service! Not having to change diapers is one of the reasons I am glad I adopted older children! I don't mean to be overly graphic, but all the feet washing and diaper changing in the world could never compare to the act of God incarnate taking on our sin.

Paul Serving the Church

It is not difficult to find countless examples of servant leadership in the Bible. Nor is it difficult to find countless examples of sinful and selfish leaders in the Bible. Two of the most notable sinful and selfish are King Ahab and Queen Jezebel! In fact, 1 Kings 16:30 says, "Ahab son of Omri did more evil in the eyes of the Lord than any of those before him." Due to the selfish, narcissistic, and sinful nature of Ahab and Jezebel, all of Israel suffered tremendously under their deception. The apostle Paul reminds us in Philippians 2:3–4, "Do nothing out of selfish ambition or vain conceit. Rather, in humility value others above yourselves, not looking to your own interests but each of you to the interests of the others."

Paul certainly reflected Christ and the attitude of servant leadership. Think of all that he gave up as a "Pharisee among Pharisees" to serve Christ and His Church. Everything that Jesus, Paul, and other servant leaders have done fits this description of discipleship: We do grow in our relationship and likeness of Christ just for our own benefit. Our growth in Christ is also for the benefit of others. This is what it means to live for the Kingdom. Notice that being formed in the image of Christ is not just for our hopes of gaining piety. Rather, it is for the sake of others. The call to be a servant leader is exactly what we must keep in mind when we have children through natural means or adoption. In fact, I have spoken to many potential adoptive parents and encouraged them to consider whether there is even the most remote hint of selfishness in their desire to adopt. Believe it or not, the desire to adopt a child because a person "has a lot of love to give" is a hint of selfishness. What will you do in the moments (and there will be a lot of them) when that child says, "I hate you," or worse, throws a string of profanities at you? Certainly, angry words from a child to a parent can happen in biological families.

Being a servant leader can make it emotionally difficult to push through behavioral challenges when our children are older. For these reasons and more, it is necessary to display servant leadership when our children are young enough to benefit from having this style of leadership as the foundation of their development. By exercising appropriate servant leadership built on trust, children and youth who experience a foundation of love have a much better chance of understanding the foundations of their core development. They receive the message, "I am loved!" When children and teens receive love, they are more easily able to reciprocate love to family and those around them in their communities. After all, shouldn't love be the core of our humanity? Remember, the greatest commandment "Jesus replied: 'love the Lord your God with all your heart and with all your soul and with all your mind.' This is the first and greatest commandment. ***And the second is like it***: 'Love your neighbor as yourself'" (Matthew 22:37–39) [emphasis added]. Jesus even declared that all the Law and the Prophets hang on these two commandments (Matthew 23:40). The truth of this commandment might indicate that even our children's development hangs on these two commandments.

Questions

1. How does servant leadership build trust between infant/toddler and parents/adults?

2. Parenting an infant or a toddler can be physically exhausting and sometimes frustrating, especially when you are sleep deprived and cannot figure out what a crying baby needs. How do you plan to have physical, spiritual, and emotional rest in order to maintain the energy being a servant leader requires?

3. Are you thinking about who can serve as a spiritual guide to your child as he or she grows?

4. What joys did you (or are you) experiencing as a parent of an infant or a toddler?

5. What support systems do you have in place for your family as you think about lifelong discipleship?

6. Are you serving well in your role as a parent or as a spouse?

7. Of all the things we will teach our children in our lifetimes, why is discipleship the most important?

Chapter 2

Leadership Model: Character

Leadership Theory

Trait Leadership and Learning Skills for Discipleship (Ages 1.5–3)

Erikson's Stage

Autonomy Versus Shame

Biblical Example: David the shepherd

"I do it!" These are the words every parent has heard from his or her preschooler! Part of letting a child know that he is loved is by allowing him to move toward healthy interdependence. In America, the national psyche has been formed by a rugged individualism. We even hear individualism in our child-raising efforts. We are told that we should raise our children to be healthy, independent adults. This independence is the opposite end of the spectrum from codependence, which is a level of reliance on others for fulfilment that can actually cause damage in relationships. However, instead of raising children who are either independent or codependent, we should be looking at raising healthy *inter*dependent adults. What this means is that we understand our actions have an impact on others.

Writing about trait leadership and skills development for such a young age can seem strange, but we all know that children often take on the traits of their parents. There are traits that children are born with. With this in mind, we want to look at trait leadership proposed by Ralph Stogdill (1948, 1974)[9] and skills leadership proposed by Robert Katz. First let us look at trait leadership and the core characteristics of that model. Trait leadership has the following characteristics: intelligence, alertness, insight, responsibility, initiative, persistence, self-confidence, and sociability. Once again, these are traits that seem to be innate in some human beings.

We know that the brains of preschoolers experience the most significant growth and development during these years (1.5–3 years). Toddler through preschool years are filled with the most concentrated learning. While the child's understanding of responsibility is minimal, they are learning the basics of responsibility by feeding themselves, potty training, dressing themselves, etc. Think about all the learning that happens between the toddler and preschool years! They learn to walk (and run), talk, receive and send social signals, engage in their environment, and so much more. Many of these types of actions are learned or *skills* acquired. Granted, some of the characteristics are limited in scope—as I mentioned, such as responsibility, insight, and self-confidence. However, it takes a tremendous amount of insight to read social cues. The ability to read social cues can be both innate (trait) or acquired (skills). Remember, I am only advocating that these characteristics are in their formative stage. While some characteristics of a child might seem innate, even characteristics children may be born with need nurturing. What is more, parents and other adults are the ones who model these characteristics to their children.

Now let us look at skills leadership put forward by Robert Katz.[10] Researchers state that some of the attributes of skills leadership are competencies, individual attributes, and environmental influences. Further, skills leadership has three different components: technical, human, and conceptual skills. Technical skills are hands-on activities, such as dressing themselves, while human skills are concepts and ideas. Conceptual skills include problem-solving, social judgment, and knowledge (Mumford, 2000).[11] Therefore, it is natural for toddlers and preschoolers to want to start doing tasks by themselves. They might want to dress themselves, pick their own food, have a choice in toys, or decide when they playfully run away. They are beginning to get a sense of self. To be clear, both trait and skills leadership are clearly defined and research focusing on adult leadership. What I am addressing here is the developmental process of trait and skills leadership as it is forming from our earliest ages.

Both trait theory and skills theory are very much leader-centric and, I know this is a bit of a stretch, but a child is learning to lead themselves and become "their own person." Of course, in this process, they need their parents to help them develop these skills. These "skills" are rudimentary, since children are learning basic skills. On the other hand, think about the number of "hands-on" skills toddlers engage in during such a short period of time. Their bodies are constantly working on coordination and becoming more self-aware of spatial interactions. Toddlers do an incredible number of actions that mimic adults. While practicing and mimicking does not mean they have obtained skills, they are learning through playing, interpreting social cues, and doing what adults do. We intuitively encourage the development of skills by saying something like, "My! Look what a big boy you have become," when a toddler does something on their own. Toddlers are constantly trying to figure out how to solve problems. They may figure out that if they push the chair up to the kitchen counter, they can get the cookie. Figuring out how to push the chair up to the kitchen counter to get what the child wants is a conceptual skill. Since these skills are at a rudimentary level, parents, grandparents, and caregivers must be the ones who model skills and trait development.

For Erik Erikson's psychosocial developmental stage two, we see the primary focus is to help a child develop autonomy versus shame. Therefore, when infants and toddlers accomplish some new task, good parents want to celebrate those tasks as milestones. Think about how excited you were when your child first sat up, took her first steps, spoke her first word, or did any number of other actions young children do. For instance, when a child dresses herself for the first time, autonomy is strengthened when the parent is complimentary of the child. If the parent is critical with a comment like, "Why did you dress that way? Your clothes do not match," or "You put your shirt on wrong," these types of messages can cause a child to have doubt in his or her autonomy and to experience shame.

Since we do not want to shame our children, giving words of encouragement that nurture regarding both trait and skills development during the first six years of a child's life are essential for development of both confidence and character development. Any parent who pays attention to their child's development will tell you that it does not take long for a child's character to be seen. The child already begins to develop a sense of self. Confident toddlers and preschoolers typically have an outgoing personality. When parents instill confidence, words of affirmation become a significant part of a child's character development as they have been "celebrated" when they reach milestones. Confidence is both a trait and a skill because confidence looks innate, that is something a child is born with, but confidence is also learned.

However, external actions are not the only type of "character" that needs to be considered. The character of a child is formed as the child reflects the values of the parent. Therefore, we must be careful about what we do and say around children because they are like sponges. They truly take a lot of information in and then repeat that information when we least expect it. Repeating adult values back to them is called "parroting." We know what parrots do; they repeat what they hear. Who hasn't been embarrassed by a child's repeating what he has heard from a parent or other caregiver? Parroting values at a young age impacts the future years where children, up through their early to mid-adolescence, take to heart what important values adults or older siblings say and display through their lives. So, if your child hears lots of affirming and truthful statements, the child will likely give out positive messages. If the child has experienced a large degree of shame, the child will be negative.

If children are encouraged in skills they learn and traits that are innate at the basic levels, children begin to develop healthier character. Parents and other adults must be careful to make sure that every child has positivity modeled to him or her. Parents will do an incredible amount of modeling throughout their child's life, and, as you can see, this modeling starts at a young age for children and never really stops. What we say, how we say it, and what we model are incredibly important for the development of our children. Modeling our faith and putting action to our words is why Deuteronomy 6:5–7 is so important because true discipleship happens "as you go." It is not complicated, but that doesn't mean it is not difficult to keep control of our tongues (James 3:1–12). Further, this is why Proverbs 22:6 is so important: "Start children off on the way they should go, and even when they are old they will not turn from it."

As an adoptive parent who has spoken to many other parents and as a minister who has worked with thousands of young people and families, kids who do not get the nurture they need will grow up to be dysfunctional and unhealthy. The character of children is formed at young ages. We have been indoctrinated by our culture to think that we *must* have a two-income home. Certainly, a two-income home does make life more comfortable. However, as a single-parent dad, I have had to be creative to make ends meet. Single-parent homes led by mothers struggle more since women are typically and unjustly paid less than men for doing the same job. We have come to a point in our culture where we have become dependent on a two-income home for comfort, security, and amenities.

Within the two-working-parent home, parents are often reliant on grandparents or other family members to raise their children. The other option is costly daycare. Most couples will tell you that most of their expenses are for childcare and gas. In other words, the extra money that comes in is often negligible. I am *not* saying that parents *need* to stay home—especially mothers. However, what I want us to think about is if character is developed in crucial ways in the first six years of a child's life, why is our culture so quick to have someone else instill their character into our children? Simply put, no one will love and nurture your child more or better than you will. Is the (negligible) extra money worth the time missed bonding with your children? Is it worth the missed opportunity to shape the character of your child? Will a childcare worker model the same character you want your child to have?

We must ask the question: "What drives my existence?" Are we driven to make more money to be "happy" or comfortable or to give more "stuff" to our children? Doesn't that drive breed further discontentment? The first two stages of Erikson's psychosocial development, trust versus mistrust and autonomy versus shame, take a great deal of interaction between parent and child. As adults, we all know that trust takes time and interaction. The more you interact with your child, the more trust you build. The more you model positive traits and skills, as well as praising your child for doing those things, the more you bond with your child. When your child sees you modeling positive actions, coming from your values, he or she will want to do those actions as well. It is then our role, as disciplers and leaders in our household, to applaud when our child attempts to act upon positive actions or live out family values.

Have you ever seen a child mimic what his parent is doing, even though the child does not have that trait? For instance, if mom or dad is reading a book or mowing the lawn, how many times do we see a child "read a book" or pretend to mow the lawn with their toy lawnmower. Children will begin acting out reading and lawn mowing at ages four to six, well before they can do them. When it comes to the value of spiritual development, do our children "read" their Bibles because they see us do it, or do they keep themselves "glued to a screen" because that is what we do? While there is no perfect parent, we must grow in our parenting skills.

We all have probably experienced times when the Internet in our home goes down. Losing our Internet connection can be incredibly frustrating—especially when we are working on something important. However, this might be a God-given opportunity to reconnect with our families through a good old-fashioned game night! What a great way to escape the allure of the screen. This also reminds us to connect with our children and families and lets them know they are important. Sometimes, we must simply disconnect from our electronics even if the Internet is up and running. With the busyness of life, we can easily get out the habit of family game night. (It is easy to get out of healthy habits and to slip into unhealthy ones.) Recently, when our Internet went down, instead of reading (which is a good option) or getting on his phone to play a downloaded game, my 15-year-old decided he wanted us to play some board games, so out came Monopoly. We had a blast! Instead of complaining that the Internet was down, my son came back to what we should have been continuing in our family life. (See how Proverbs 22:6 comes into play?) During earlier years of my kids' lives, I had modeled the concept of family game night to my children. Now that my kids are older, they often model back to me the need to disconnect from the Internet and reconnect with each other.

When our children are one and a half to three years of age, what we model, how often we model it, and how consistently we model it begin that crucial process of character formation in our children. Remember, from the birth of our children to the time they are one and a half years old, Christ and his servant leadership are the things we should focus on with them. Modeling Christ does not go away or diminish as our children grow and mature. In fact, the need for showing Christ-like servant leadership to our children continues throughout our lives. When our children are one and a half to three years of age, we are simply adding another tool to our tool belt.

Biblical Example of Trait and Skills Leadership

The biblical example of trait and skills leadership to disciple can be found in the example of David. Most of us are aware of David, the second king of Israel. There are some important things we need to know about David. David was a skilled shepherd, and it was these skills that God used to defeat Goliath and the Philistines. David had been a shepherd most of his life. Since David had multiple older brothers and since most Jewish boys learned the trades of their fathers, it would not be a wild speculation to assume that David had been learning how to be a shepherd at a young age. David began to develop technical skills. He learned certain "shepherd" traits from his family. However, David also developed conceptual skills; this is a fact that must not be overlooked.

Not only did David have the technical skills to kill the bear and the lion (1 Samuel 17:36) and to use these skills against Goliath, the Philistines, and the other enemies of Israel, but David also gained conceptual skills by choosing to use his sling rather than face Goliath in hand-to-hand combat—which was what the much larger Goliath expected.

David displayed his conceptual skills, which, as we recall, involve problem-solving, social judgment, and knowledge. David mastered these attributes well because we see how his ability to "read the room" kept him from being harmed by Jonathan's murderous father, King Saul. Problem solving, social judgment, and knowledge are personality skills developed at a young age. In 1 Samuel 17, David had a heart that was willing to tend to the sheep of his father, Jesse. Further, David had an incredibly reverential heart for God. These internal traits were both innate and further developed. Even though Saul was attempting to kill David, David refused to retaliate against Saul when the opportunity presented itself and David could have taken Saul's life. Not only did David refrain from taking Saul's life, but David also did not want to offend God (1 Samuel 24:6). Character traits of deep friendship, loyalty, trusting in God were attributes that deeply abided in David's character.

In the scope of life, we have so little time to develop godly character within our children. We must take advantage of every moment to develop godly character in our children because when as children age, developing godly character can become much more difficult. This is why, as parents, we must model godly character and strengthen these attributes within our children. At Toccoa Falls College (TFC) where I am a professor, the motto is, "Developing [godly] character with intellect." I love the fact that one can face a rigorous academic environment and still retain godly character. Even though TFC is a Christian college, not every student that goes to TFC is a believer. One thing that is difficult to ignore is the intentionality of building a community, based on godly character, among our students. When students are asked why they chose TFC, the most common response is "the sense of community." This is not by accident. The entire college faculty and staff work hard to model godly character and help to cultivate that same character within our students. This is the same way it must be with our children; we must model traits and skills early for our children so such goldy attributes become a part of their character.

One of my son's (and my) favorite songs is by Rodney Atkins called, "I've Been Watching You." It is a powerful song about the role of parents modeling behaviors to their children. Through the good and the bad behaviors modeled by the dad, the song epitomizes how our children look up to us and mimic our behaviors. I encourage you to search for the song and read the words of the four-year-old child in the song. You will find a wonderful illustration of what it means to practice trait leadership. When it comes to leading children during their early childhood years, we want to make sure that we are displaying the traits of great biblical leaders and avoiding the bad traits of bad leaders. The truth is that there is not a clear delineation between "nature vs. nurture" when it comes to raising children because our children are impacted both by how we raise them (nurture) and who God has created them to be (nature). I cannot emphasize this enough: your children learn by the traits of your character allowing them to nurture the character God has given them.

Questions

1. How do you see your traits and characteristics begin to display themselves through the lives of your young children (or grandchildren)?

2. How do you see your child's personality beginning to develop?

3. What skills do you see developing? How do you appropriately celebrate milestones?

4. What discipleship practices can you model to your children at this young age?

5. How does nurturing their innate traits help your child understand that he or she is loved?

6. How does discipleship take on intentionality even at this age?

7. Have you and your spouse (or another support person) discussed how to develop an intentional discipleship and leadership plan? What could that plan potentially look like?

Compassion Years

"I Belong to God"

(Ages 3–12)

Chapter 3

Leadership Model: Cop

Leadership Theory

Transactional Leadership (Ages 3–6)

Erikson's Stage

Initiative Versus Guilt   Biblical Example: David and Nathan

My son Jamie pointed out to me that the Los Angeles Police Department coined their official motto "To Protect and Serve" in 1955.[12] You will see the value of that motto shortly. This section of the book moves beyond the strong foundation of the core development years that lets a child know that the child is loved. The next stage moves on to building the foundations of compassion and letting the child know he or she "belongs." From ages three to six, children are moving away from the heavily ego-driven self to the foundations based in belonging. Their world is not just their immediate surroundings of the self. Now, they begin to understand they are part of a family. When a child moves through the ages of three to six, they need to know boundaries and that they belong to a community. This is where parents spend a great deal of time teaching their children right from wrong and helping the child develop compassion for others. It is for this reason that I propose using transactional leadership as a part of discipleship. Admittedly, transactional leadership is one of the least favored models of leadership.

One basic way of understanding transactional leadership in the work world is where an employer pays an employee for the work she has done. Practicing transactional leadership can thus assume an understanding of actions leading to reward (or consequence). At a basic level, transactional can be exemplified by a vending machine. If a product costs $1, you put your money in the machine intending to get a certain product in return. There is little human emotion involved, unless the machine does not give you what you paid for. It is easy to see why transactional leadership is one of the least preferred models of leadership and yet, there is a place for this model.

I need to reiterate that leadership models can overlap. For instance, when your child begins elementary school, there may still be a need for servant leadership and for you to model Christ. The need for Christ to be modeled never goes away, it simply now overlaps as character continues to be developed. Transactional leadership works well with children ages three to six because there is a need for a higher degree of structure (provided by the parent) while implementing systems of rewards and consequences. One way to think about it is that transactional leadership takes on more of the duties and strategies of a "cop."

Transactional leadership is often based on a reward system.[13] In other words, when children make good choices, we often reward them for their choices, whether that is a good grade in school or an ice-cream cone for good behavior. Transactional leadership as a way of discipling our children is not as mechanical as the vending machine illustration. In other words, positive reinforcement is a system that managers use to motivate followers because it is in the followers' best interest to comply. For teachers, especially in elementary school, transactional leadership is a way of organizing and controlling lessons and managing the classroom. Often, children are rewarded for positive behaviors. On the other hand, children might often face consequences for inappropriate behavior. For instance, a child who misbehaves or does not complete an assignment might be deprived of recess or some other fun activity. Transactional leadership often appeals to a child because a child is driven by self-interests as they are egocentric. As you can see, transactional leadership is helpful for young children.

As children become more mobile and independent, the need for more guidance is obvious. The continued need for parental guidance is especially true as a child begins to engage in social interactions beyond the home. As a child expands their world beyond the family, the child will need to understand the cause and effect of their decisions on relationships both inside and outside the home. The leader is responsible for maintaining a routine to assist in how the follower functions. Since children are concrete thinkers, there is an understanding that "if you do this action, then this result will happen." Some of the results can be natural. For instance, "since you did not do your homework, you received a bad grade." Other results can be more of an understanding. "If you do your chores, you will receive an allowance."

For Erikson's psychosocial development, ages three to six go through the stage of initiative versus guilt. For this age, socialization with others outside the family takes place. Learning to socialize involves interacting with others in ways that are fair, empathetic, and abiding by socially accepted behaviors. We live in a society where children are forced to grow up too quickly through gaining competence rather than simply being children by learning through play. You may have heard of videos that push young children academically or in sports rather than letting them just be children and learn naturally through social interaction and play. Play is where children not only learn socialization, but they also learn the rules of games, learn to follow instructions, and even learn empathy. Children can also develop initiative and imagination. Several recent books emphasize the importance of play for children. For some great insight on the need for play, I recommend *The Power of Play* by Dr. David Elkind (2007) and *The Anxious Generation* by Jonathan Haidt (2024).

It may seem counterintuitive to use the image of a "cop" to describe a parent's role for this stage of life as described by Erikson. However, we must remember what the roles of police personnel are. "Cops" keep the order and help prevent chaos. Police enforce the rules by issuing consequences such as tickets, jail, etc., and while these consequences seem negative, can you imagine what the world would be like without good police officers? As I mentioned in the opening sentence of this chapter, the motto of many police force operations is "To Protect and Serve." Do we not want to protect and serve our children? Of course, we do! We protect by telling our children, "Don't touch the hot stove." We teach them the rules to keep them and others safe. If our child tries to take a toy from another child through force, we correct them. Transactional leadership fits perfectly into the psychosocial development that Erikson describes. The positive aspects of "policing" are where we want to focus. We want to teach our children how to act with others, thereby helping them to understand interdependence. We are teaching that our actions impact each other,

I asked a rhetorical question a few lines ago: "Can you imagine what the world would look like without good police officers?" I will assume you are, like most, a good, law-abiding citizen. However, if we are honest, if we know we can get away with going over the speed limit, how many of us will push that limit if we know there are no police around? (Be honest!) Police officers are there to keep us safe and serve as a sort of "visible conscience" when we might be tempted to do something that we should not. Remember, transactional leadership is based on the principle of "if you do a certain action, then a certain reaction will happen." The truth is, that if we typically do what is good, we can expect good consequences. If we do something bad, we can expect bad consequences. The years of three to six are crucial years for understanding how to interact well with others.

Now, if you become a "bad cop" in that you are always criticizing your child, you stand a good chance of crushing their spirit. There is a big difference between guiding the will of a child or crushing their spirit. Crushing their spirit is the opposite of being a "good cop." A good cop enforces the rules so the community can function and accept each other. Without guidance and enforcing rules, the community can easily slip into chaos! This chaos would come from everybody acting without consequences. When chaos happens, people begin to get excluded from a safe community and they also begin to exclude others. In fact, "transactional leadership" is all over the Bible when it comes to following the rules and the consequences that happen when we don't follow the rules.

Consider Adam and Eve. God gave Adam and Eve an abundance of choices of what they could eat, except from the one tree in the middle of the garden. Look at the account in Genesis 2:15–17:

> The Lord God took the man and put him in the Garden of Eden to work it and take care of it. And the Lord God commanded the man, "You are free to eat from any tree in the garden; but you must not eat from the tree of the knowledge of good and evil, for when you eat from it you will certainly die."

God clearly gave Adam a rule and, even though the rule may have been given before Eve was created, there is an indication that Eve had been informed about which fruit to eat and which to avoid. Eve recited the command in Genesis 3:2–3 saying, "The woman said to the serpent, 'We may eat fruit from the trees in the garden, but God did say, 'You must not eat fruit from the tree that is in the middle of the garden, and you must not touch it, or you will die.'"

I must divert, for just a moment, to observe an overlooked aspect of teaching in the first chapter of Genesis that should be abundantly clear. In Genesis 1:28, Scripture tells us, "God blessed them [Adam and Eve] and said to them, 'Be fruitful and increase in number; fill the earth and subdue it. Rule over the fish in the sea and the birds in the sky and over every living creature that moves on the ground.'" Notice that God did not tell Adam and Eve simply to "increase in number." No, there is the command prior to increasing and that command is to be "fruitful." This is important. To be fruitful, such as taking care of the earth, a person requires good judgment. Good judgment and making wise choices lead to a fruitful life. When we have a fruitful life that is filled with wisdom, we pass these characteristics on to our children. When we follow the rules and set that example, we have a better likelihood that our children will follow the rules. Having this pattern of behavior generation after generation leads us to being "fruitful and multiplying."

Genesis 2 records the instructions God gave about what Adam and Eve could and could not eat. You already know that they had a lot open to them to eat, but they just had to go for the one tree God said not to touch! (Isn't that just like human nature?) We know the rest of the story. Eve, and then Adam, succumbed to temptation. Notice what Satan did though to deceive Eve with these words in Genesis 3:4–5, "'You will not certainly die,' the serpent said to the woman. 'For God knows that when you eat from it your eyes will be opened, and you will be like God, knowing good and evil.'"

First, Satan outright lied. We know that the results of poor choices lead to bad consequences. In this case, the wages of sin is death (Romans 6:23a). Second, Satan told a partial truth. Notice he said, "You will be like God, knowing good and evil." I find it interesting that Satan did not say, "You will be like God, knowing ***the difference*** *between* good and evil." In fact, Satan's words ring out to be true because Adam and Eve ***knew evil*** when Cain killed Abel! Now, we begin to see a pattern of natural consequences. In other words, we begin to see what happens when we do not live a fruitful life (of wisdom) and then multiply (not only in children, but in poor decisions). There is a litany of natural consequences that happen once Adam and Even rebelled against God's created order.

- In God's mercy, Adam and Eve were removed from the garden. The removal is merciful because, had Adam and Eve eaten from the tree of eternal life *after* eating from the tree in the middle of the garden, they would have been eternally separated from God in their sin (Genesis 3:22).

- Since Adam was created from the dust and, since he was to work the ground, the ground was cursed thereby making his work more difficult. In the end, his body would return to the ground (Genesis 3:17–19).
- Since Eve was created from Adam and his flesh, her childbirth experience (flesh from flesh) would increase in pain (Genesis 3:16).
- Of course, there is a consequence for Satan as well. The consequence for Satan presents the first prophecy of Jesus as Messiah who would come to save us from our sin (Genesis 3:15).

We need to lead our children with a transactional leadership model. Giving consequences or rewards goes to the fact that we must help them understand that their actions impact others and there are natural consequences for both good (fruitful) and bad choices. It should also be noted that what Adam and Eve desired and envied became exponentially devastating when Cain killed Abel. While Adam and Eve's decision did not lead to immediate death, Cain's decision did. I often say, "What parents do in moderation their children will take to excess!" I should be clear that, as a parent, you cannot always wait for "natural consequences." For instance, it would be cruel and inhumane not to immediately jump in and stop a child from touching a hot stove. We cannot have the mentality, "Well, that will teach them!" There are times when we must step in and apply consequences for the good of our child! If we do not, we are abandoning the discipline in the word *disciple* (Proverbs 3:12; Hebrews 12:6).

So, if we are going to disciple our children through transactional leadership and help them to see that good decisions have a better potential for positive outcomes, we must make sure we follow the rules as well. We cannot say, "Do as I say, not as I do." To say one thing and do the opposite is called hypocrisy. If you have ever had an older child who is about to start driving and they let you know that you are going over the speed limit, it is amazing how quickly you want to be more careful about obeying speed limits and traffic laws! Young people are good at sniffing out hypocrisy! Leadership requires us to do what we also expect of others.

When I lead my children, congregation, or college students, I do not ask them to do an action or assignment I am not willing to do myself. It does not matter if the task is cleaning a toilet or leading a small group, I want to lead by example. The concept of living a fruitful life can be found by following God's precepts, obeying the speed limits, not watching or listening to harmful movies or music, or serving others. I know that if I follow wisdom, if I am fruitful, then fruitful consequences will follow. Having consequences is also true of making unwise decisions. If I make poor decisions, I can expect negative consequences. I am thankful, however, for 1 John 1:8–9, "If we claim to be without sin, we deceive ourselves and the truth is not in us. If we confess our sins, he is faithful and just and will forgive us our sins and purify us from all unrighteousness."

Part of understanding transactional leadership is taking ownership of our shortcomings. We do not blame others for our mistakes. Notice that in Genesis 3:12–13, Adam and Eve both began shifting the blame for the consequences of their decisions. Adam went so far as to insinuate that his poor decision was somehow both God's and Eve's fault. Listen to his words: "The man said, 'The woman you put here with me—she gave me some fruit from the tree, and I ate it'" (Genesis 3:12). We can have a process in our home when it comes to transactional leadership and making mistakes. Our five-step process is this: 1) admit your mistake, 2) apologize and seek forgiveness from the one you harmed, 3) try to make it right through corrective action, 4) learn from your mistake, and finally, 5) move on.

The process of reconciliation and ownership of mistakes communicates the message that your child still belongs to you, no matter what mistakes they make. Reconciliation also communicates the fact that your children also belong to God. When we use discipline as a loving discipleship process, we guide children closer to the truths of God's teachings. It is easy to overlook the following verse in 3 John 1:4, "I have no greater joy than to hear that my children are walking in the truth."

We live in a world that says there is no absolute truth (which, ironically, is an absolute truth claim). However, when I tell my children, "I love you," that is an absolute truth claim! Even more so, when God tells His children He loves them, it is an absolute truth claim! Maybe we need to meditate on this word in Romans 5:8: "But God demonstrates his own love for us in this: **While we were still sinners**, Christ died for us" [emphasis added]. We have a false theology when there is not allowed to be any spiritual discipline going on in the church. This false theology comes out in the statement, "You can't judge me!" It is true that we cannot jump to conclusions and falsely make judgments. However, discerning whether someone is living a life that honors God while claiming to be a Christian is one of the reasons the epistles are given to Christians! The epistles are letters defining godly living. If we were not supposed to help each other be accountable to a godly life, we might as well ignore all the Epistles!

The letters in the Bible are there for the very reason of correcting, and they were written to believers, not to the world!

Paul wrote in 1 Corinthians 5:12, "What business is it of mine to judge those outside the church? Are you not to judge those inside?" Today, we have it backward. "Church folks" are judging the world while they themselves are engaging in all kinds of egregious behaviors! Also remember the admonishment in 2 Timothy 3:16–17, "All Scripture is God-breathed and is useful for teaching, rebuking, correcting and training in righteousness, so that the servant of God may be thoroughly equipped for every good work." The entire book of James is written as the New Testament book of wisdom. The book of James, and all the Epistles, tell us how Christians ought to live a godly life.

Discipline (the root word of *disciple*) *is* leadership! While we want to "play nice," correction is often necessary. Remember, Jesus called the Pharisees children of the devil (John 8:44) and a brood of vipers (Matthew 12:34), and He rebuked Peter by saying, "Get behind me, Satan" (Mathew 16:23). John the Baptist called the Pharisees a brood of vipers (Matthew 3:7), and 1 John 3:10 states, "This is how we know who the children of God are and who the children of the devil are: Anyone who does not do what is right is not God's child, nor is anyone who does not love their brother and sister." Bad pop culture theology says, "We're all God's children!" No, we are not, and to project this false message against the truth claims of the Bible puts a person who believes this under Satan's influence.

Nobody likes to play "bad cop," but because bad theology is so pervasive in our churches, the importance of discipline and discipleship have been minimized! I am not advocating that you call your children "children of the devil"! That won't get you anywhere. I am advocating that, if we want our children to grow up understanding truth, we need to raise them up knowing right and wrong based on the truth claims of Scripture. You cannot live by the truth of the world and by the truth of Scripture (1 John 2:15), and you cannot serve two Masters (Matthew 6:24). Are you beginning to see how important your role in discipleship is? Children will learn how to navigate life and gain wisdom through your practice of transactional leadership as you point out truth and lies. As I mentioned before, children can sniff out hypocrisy a mile away! We must practice what we preach!

Biblical Examples of Transactional Leadership

In today's increasingly secular culture, and among biblically illiterate churchgoers, it may be good to remind everyone of an account of King David, a man after God's own heart. The whole context can be found in 2 Samuel chapters 11–12, but here is a quick summary: David was not where he should be. Instead of leading the army, one spring, David stayed back in the palace. As he was on the palace roof, David saw Bathsheba bathing and, instead of turning away, he entertained lustful thoughts. He used his influence to have sex with Bathsheba while her husband, Uriah, was away at war. Bathsheba became pregnant. David connived in all kinds of ways to bring Uriah back from battle and hoped he would sleep with Bathsheba. Uriah was a man of principle and would not allow himself the pleasure of home comforts while his men were at the battlefield away from their families. When David's planning didn't work, he had Uriah killed in battle.

Then Nathan the prophet came along and told David a short, and believable story in 2 Samuel 12:1–4:

> The Lord sent Nathan to David. When he came to him, he said, "There were two men in a certain town, one rich and the other poor. The rich man had a very large number of sheep and cattle, but the poor man had nothing except one little ewe lamb he had bought. He raised it, and it grew up with him and his children. It shared his food, drank from his cup and even slept in his arms. It was like a daughter to him. Now a traveler came to the rich man, but the rich man refrained from taking one of his own sheep or cattle to prepare a meal for the traveler who had come to him. Instead, he took the ewe lamb that belonged to the poor man and prepared it for the one who had come to him.

David was livid and he pronounced his own judgment on himself:

> David burned with anger against the man and said to Nathan, "As surely as the Lord lives, the man who did this must die! He must pay for that lamb four times over, because he did such a thing and had no pity" (2 Samuel 12:5–6).

In his confrontation with David, Nathan had to be the "bad cop." He told David outright, "You are that man!" Nathan pronounced God's judgment against David. Notice what happens next, for these are the responses of David that keep him as a "man after God's own heart." First, David repented and admitted that he had sinned. He recognized that he sinned against God, Uriah, and Bathsheba. He tried to atone for his sins. (He could have left Bathsheba out in the cold, but he took her into the palace.) David learned (the hard way) from his mistakes, and he moved on. (Does this process of reconciliation sound familiar from a few pages ago?) What you will also notice, though, is that David still had to face the consequences of his sin. David lost his child with Bathsheba, there was gross sexual immorality among his children, and one of his sons tried to overthrow him. As bad as all these situations sound, can you imagine what David and his kingdom would have been like had God not restored the relationship?

There are several other examples of transactional leadership in the Bible: Jesus' healing the invalid (John 5:1–9), Peter's healing the lame man (Acts 3:1–10), and Jesus' forgiving the adulterous woman (John 8:1–11). In each of these stories, there is the concept that "if this, then that." Consistently throughout both the Old and the New Testaments, there is the concept that "if you obey my commands," then there will usually be blessings to follow. In the New Testament, Jesus told the disciples the world will know we are His disciples if we obey His commands. Even though David "messed up" in a big way, he truly attempted to obey God's commands. It was the position of his heart to repent when he acknowledged his sin.

Here is the thing—even after all the mess David created, he still belonged to God! God's love is not transactional—His love is unconditional. This should be great news for you, me, our children, and our grandchildren. First John 3:1 states it well, "See what great love the Father has lavished on us, that we should be called children of God! And that is what we are! The reason the world does not know us is that it did not know him." Those who refuse the persistent and unconditional love of God do not know what they are missing! While we may be playing the role of "cop," our job is to protect and serve so our children will always know they belong no matter what! Just as Jesus promises us that no one can snatch us out of His hands (John 10:29), we need to let our children, grandchildren, and other children know they belong to God!

Questions

1. How does establishing boundaries and wise decisions communicate to our children that they have a sense of belonging?

2. What happens socially when children do not have boundaries?

3. How can you begin developing a generous and compassionate heart within your child?

4. Extended family (grandparents, aunts, uncles, and the like) are the next level of social interactions your child learns from. If you do not have extended family living close by, who can fill those roles for your children and help disciple them?

5. In the hectic pace of life, how are you being intentional in spending your time with your child?

6. How can your church fill some of these roles?

7. Why is church involvement, as a family, important?

8. At what age do you think a child should decide whether he or she goes to church with you or not? Why?

Chapter 4

Discipleship Model: Coach

Leadership Theory

Path-Goal Leadership (Ages 6–12)

Erikson's Stage

Industry Versus Inferiority

Biblical Example: Moses and Jethro

Leadership expert Robert House is the main theorist of the path-goal model of leadership.[14] He developed this theory in 1971 and revised it in 1996. Path-goal leadership is about helping a follower discover more about themselves. This approach puts followers' needs first through motivational factors. In this case, your leadership is in the organization of your family while coaching your children through motivational factors. Path-goal theory allows the leader the opportunity to help followers define goals, clarify paths, remove obstacles, and provide support for the follower, while leader behaviors are typically directive, supportive, participative, or achievement oriented. There are two different types of path-goal leadership objectives: directive leadership is one form of leadership used for low-skill followers while supportive leadership grows confidence in a follower. Whether directive or supportive, path-goal leadership is participative, allowing for collaboration, but it also encourages achievement and, therefore, places a high standard on a follower who can excel.

Here are some of the strengths when it comes to path-goal leadership. Leaders can adjust according to the needs of the follower. While some leaders may have natural abilities toward trait, skills, or even servant leadership, path-goal leaders can be trained in path-goal approaches to coaching. If you think about it, most coaches had someone teaching them how to coach. Another strength in path-goal leadership is that it integrates motivation of the follower. If my sons are motivated to play a sport or to learn a new skill, their motivation is what allows me to set markers that help them achieve their goal. One significant way we can help our children set goals is when our children want to start earning their own money. A child is more motivated to accomplish chores when they are motivated, not by money, but by the item they might want to buy with the money they have earned. I would much rather teach my sons that working toward a goal is better than just having it handed to them. Further, path-goal leadership brings clarity for the follower while removing any potential obstacles to achieving the goal. Bringing clarity and showing potential obstacles is another way coaching comes in to play. If our children see obstacles, instead of bulldozing the obstacle for our children, we can coach them on how to overcome the obstacle. We have literally moved from the concept of "helicopter parents" to "snowplow parents." By removing struggles from the lives of our children, we are not helping them build resilience, and it takes a great deal of resilience to engage in the spiritual process of sanctification. There is a significant difference between helping our children see potential obstacles and removing them. By coaching our children through the path-goal leadership approach, we allow opportunities for their personal growth.

Erikson's psychosocial development stage for this age group is called "industry versus inferiority" (Erikson, 1950).[15] In this particular stage of life, children and early adolescents begin to value their peers' input and seek approval. As children move from childhood to early adolescence, this truth of peer approval and belonging becomes even more apparent as some children don't want to be seen with a parent when being dropped off at school. During the stage of industry versus inferiority, we want to remind our child that his identity is found in belonging to God. It is good for us to remember as parents that when our child "slights" us while being around their peers, they are not rejecting us in so much as they do not want to be rejected by their peers.

The transition from being cop to coach, which primarily happens in the teen years, can be a challenge. As our children grow and mature, they are moving from a concrete-thinking mind where everything is black and white to a mind that is developing abstract thinking skills. With abstract thinking, they begin to discover that rules are not always black and white. We must lean into, and trust, that we have enough of a voice of wisdom that we can move from being a cop to someone who now coaches. To make the move from cop to coach, we must allow our children to have opportunities to put into practice what they have learned. Our role as coaches is now about helping our children gain competency in what they do. We are also moving beyond what are simply "right or wrong" decisions to what are the wisest decisions. We must allow our children to have options in making decisions. By allowing them to succeed or fail "safely" by giving recommendations rather than mandates, children learn how to make wise choices.

Directive path-goal leadership is especially helpful for younger children who are just entering the process of making decisions. At age six, guided choices children make are of less consequence than at age 12. A six-year-old might choose what they want to make for lunch or what type of outfit they want to wear to school. These are usually harmless decisions. A six-year-old might get teased by their peers if they wear something slightly out of the norm, but this does not need to have life-long consequences. However, for a 10- to 12-year-old, deciding whether to watch pornography on a friend's smartphone or to smoke a cigarette can have serious consequences. While there may be a need to slip back into transactional leadership if your child is consistently making poor choices, we want to continue to move toward path-goal leadership and always retain a servant leadership mindset.

Think about the role of coaching. Coaching is less about doing and more about showing someone how to accomplish a goal or a skill. Coaching is about teaching athletes and then letting them show their skills without the coach on the field with them. For years, I taught and coached both martial arts and soccer. My oldest son, Aaron, played football and took martial arts from me. I knew nothing about coaching football, but I studied martial arts most of my life and have a black belt. The sports I did not know how to coach, such as football, I left to a recognized football coach. For martial arts, however, Aaron studied with me. I was able to coach my middle son, Dylan, through six seasons of soccer. My youngest son, Jamie, enjoys reading, writing, and golf. I do my best to model reading and help him with his writing, but I am not good at golf, so I want to ensure he can get some golf lessons from a professional. As I wrote in *Voices,* the importance of seeking out mentors who can invest in our children is essential so such mentors can bring different perspectives, skills, and wisdom into the lives of our children. The need to have a number of coaches and mentors is especially true when it comes to instilling biblical wisdom and godly character into our children. Having other Christ-like people in the lives of my children helps to solidify godly character—which is much more important than sports or other skills.

When each of my sons executed a particular skill that I had taught them, you can imagine how proud I was of them. We are just as proud when our children master a skill, even when someone else coaches them. We are proud when our children get A's, score goals, or gain confidence in singing, dancing, or acting in a play. When it comes to path-goal leadership and Erikson's psychosocial development, it is best to follow this pattern when teaching our children new concepts. First, model the behavior or skill. Second, practice the behavior or skill with your child. Third, have your child practice the behavior or skill on their own. As a part of their practice, ask your child to evaluate what went well and what could have gone better. (Always praise the positive aspects of what your child did before making corrections.) Fourth, show and model the correction. Fifth, have the child continue to practice the behavior or skill complimenting what he or she is doing well. Finally, once the behavior or skill has been mastered, allow the child to continue along with gradually fading monitoring. Good coaches can work themselves out of a job.

When I taught martial arts, I always followed this process. Strengths and weaknesses would become apparent through competition. The same is true when it comes to discipleship. When engaging in discipleship, a follower should not find learning difficult. I am not going to ask my children to write a ten-page paper on Habakkuk. Remember, discipleship is an "as you go" mentality (Deuteronomy 6:4–9; Matthew 28:16–20). Reading the Bible together, asking questions about what your child got out of the reading, and asking how the passage made them feel can model life-long discipleship practices. Let your children ask questions. If the passage is difficult and you do not know an answer to a particular question, make a commitment to find the answer together. When it came to martial arts, soccer, or writing, I was always proud when my sons excelled beyond my abilities!

I cannot assume the meaning of "path-goal" leadership is apparent. Think about what coaches do as described in the previous section above. With a certain goal in mind, a coach will break the goal into a sequence of skills, creating a path toward the goal. There are two significant weaknesses that we must be aware of when it comes to path-goal leadership. The first is the complexity in the motivational factors with a follower. We may not always know what motivates our children, and what might motivate one of our children may not motivate the other. Not knowing what motivates someone makes it necessary for the leader to be adept in this area. Truly getting to know someone is where incarnational ministry comes in. We must spend quality time with our children, and by doing so, we know what motivates them. A second weakness of path-goal leadership is that instructions are mostly unidirectional coming from the leader. Dictatorial pronouncements can go against Erikson's model of "industry" in the sense that we need to allow our children to have some say in their development. Learning to engage in conversation is where coaching and feedback come in handy. Frankly, there have been times where my sons have taught me a new and better way of doing a task. In fact, if my sons do find a better way of completing a task, I applaud that. Positive affirmation is needed since the primary task Erikson describes is industry versus inferiority.

There is one more important word I need to say about coaching. We have all seen "that parent" in the stands. The parent who lives vicariously through the performance of their child on the field. The parent truly believes they are encouraging their child to "do better," but the child's spirit can get crushed by the stinging words of the parent. I had a rule when it came to coaching my sons. If I had another coach or instructor with me, the rule was that "I will correct your child, and you correct mine." Removing myself directly as my child's coach was especially helpful because, let's face it, we tend to be harder on our own kids. By being "that negative parent," we are feeding into the inferiority complex of our children. Our "coaching" can easily turn into our children feeling like they will never be able to please us. In fact, when it came to coaching my children on how to drive a stick shift car, I had other adults teach my kids. "Momma Brenda" coached my middle child to drive a stick because I knew the mentoring relationship they had was one where Momma Brenda would not be easily frustrated by my son's stalling the car (for the twelfth time), which is yet another reason to encourage mentoring outside the home.

Biblical Example of Path-Goal Leadership

One of our biblical examples of path-goal leadership comes from an interaction between Moses and his father-in-law, Jethro. If you are in any leadership position, you know how exhausting it can be. Exhaustion can be a real concern when it comes to parenting. After I became a parent, I realized that parenting was the most challenging and rewarding endeavor I had ever done in my life! I have accomplished some challenging goals and tasks in my life, but being a parent is the most challenging because there is so much emotion tied to parenting, and the stakes are incredibly high! However, when my children naturally do something good that has been "coached" in them, observing this change toward positive behaviors is rewarding! Can you imagine being in Moses' sandals and having to "parent" over two million people? We must remember that, when the Israelites were in slavery to Egypt, they did not have much coaching going on in their lives. After 400 years of being told what to do and after being given predominantly menial tasks, the Israelites knew very little about how to take care of themselves. In fact, Moses—through God's provision—pretty much had to take care of every single physical, emotional, and spiritual need the Israelites had. Talk about being exhausted!

In Exodus 18, Jethro came to the wilderness for a family visit. Jethro had been told of all the great miracles of deliverance God had done for the Israelites (Exodus 18:1, 9). Moses and Jethro had a time of catching up, fellowship, and worship (Exodus 18:7–12). Jethro's visit was going well, until verse 13. Moses had been so used to being the person where "the buck stopped" and was wearing himself out. Listen to Jethro's words in verse 14:

> When his father-in-law saw all that Moses was doing for the people, he said, "What is this you are doing for the people? Why do you alone sit as judge, while all these people stand around you from morning till evening?"

Some people say that leadership is a lonely position. Most of the time this saying is true only because, like Moses, we have made it lonely! Loneliness and exhaustion are especially true in the church when pastors fail to equip and release people for ministry. In fact, we should not be equipping people to do our ministry as pastors; we should be equipping people to do the ministry God has called them to do!

If we are investing in those we lead, whether congregation members or our own children, so they accomplish only our goals, we are engaging in systemic abandonment. Frankly, being the only authority in leadership or the home is a narcissistic way to run a ministry or our families. Yes, there are times when we can share common goals that we all move toward, but more thriving ministries and families help others live into their giftings and callings. If not, we are simply living vicariously through those we have been called to be in ministry with. In fact, one of the reasons the church in the West is struggling is that leadership has often been too centralized with the "lead pastor" who is trying to build their own ministry. For some lead pastors, the mentality is "my way or the highway." I have seen authoritarian leadership in parents as well. Being the only voice that demands its way is not a path-goal leadership model, and it certainly is not a good discipleship practice that will grow and mature our children.

Fortunately, Jethro not only pointed out the flaw of how Moses was operating but also let him know it was not healthy for Moses or the people. What Jethro observed was not about "right or wrong";

rather the input given was about wisdom. Listen again to what Jethro said as he coached Moses:

> Moses' father-in-law replied, "What you are doing is not good. You and these people who come to you will only wear yourselves out. The work is too heavy for you; you cannot handle it alone. Listen now to me and I will give you some advice, and may God be with you. You must be the people's representative before God and bring their disputes to him" (Exodus 18:17–19).

Notice that Jethro was concerned about what was best for both Moses and the people of Israel. Not only did he not diminish Moses' leadership, he was complimentary and offered a much-needed different perspective. In other words, he was rewarding what Moses had been doing. Jethro also reprioritized the necessary work of Moses and taught Moses a key leadership role—delegation! In other words, by taking Jethro's coaching, Moses became a more effective and efficient leader. Moses needed to focus on the big picture and let others help with the day-to-day "smaller stuff." Every person, from youth pastor to parent, needs to learn these truths!

Like Jethro's coaching Moses, our goal is to allow our children, as well as others we lead, to move toward interdependence, not independence or codependence! The people of Israel had become too codependent upon Moses. (Moses had unwittingly become a bulldozer parent.) With so many challenges, day in and day out, it is no wonder Moses acted out in anger and struck a rock instead of speaking to it to get water to come from it. God had clearly told Moses to speak to the rock (Numbers 20). Anger and frustration are what happens when we do not function with wisdom. We become burned out, we get frustrated, and then we act in a way that is not from God. Therefore, resting is also an essential part of reaching goals. No sport, task, or goal is worth sacrificing our well-being and mental health, as Moses was doing.

One student whom I had been training in tae kwon do, Brandon, had been training for many years. To be good at martial arts, a student must practice at least three times a week at the gym, along with even more practice at home. After several years of training, Brandon had received his black belt. I taught a more "Americanized" version of tae kwon do that allowed strikes to the side of the head with hands. Brandon was exceptionally talented, and he and I created a goal for him to complete in the Junior Olympics. After the first six months of training for the more traditional tae kwon do competition, it became apparent that Brandon was getting burned out. Sensing impending burnout, I talked to Brandon and his dad and recommended that Brandon take a three-month respite. Some people would fear that the student might not come back, but I knew that, deep down, Brandon loved the sport. Near the end of the three-month respite, Brandon was itching to get involved again. We trained for another six months and went through the competition; Brandon won the 13-year-old black belt championship for the State of Georgia in 2000. If someone wants to win bad enough, they may need a break and some rest, but they will come back even more motivated.

We have another damaging pop-culture theology that says, "Idle hands are the devil's workshop." In response, we have overprogrammed our kids and have kept them so busy that they are burning out and facing unprecedented amounts of anxiety. Many of our children and youth push forward to please helicopter parents. Don't get me wrong; sometimes our children need some external motivation, but the best motivation comes from what they have within. The same is true with "snowplow" parents. If there is no motivation to push through challenges, kids will let you do it for them.

Path-goal not only helps our children and youth see clear steps toward a goal but also engages them in a process of industry, in learning and coaching environments that allow them to be creative in accomplishing goals. As they accomplish goals, they gain a sense of belonging in a variety of opportunities. Giving ownership of ministry to students and families is why churches need to move away from youth ministries that are highly program and entertainment driven. If we are going to insist that "youth are the future of the church," we need to be equipping them for leadership as soon as possible. We need to set steps toward a goal. For instance, if we want young people to be leading worship in the future as a part of a team, as soon as a young person shows an interest in playing an instrument or singing, we should partner them with adults in the worship team so they can begin to develop in those areas. The same goes for us pastors. We need to allow young people to develop in speaking and preaching with more than just the obligatory "Youth Sunday" once a year. Path-goal leadership allows a child to engage in the concept of industry. Yes, it will take time for the skill to develop, but having a pathway to development, with all its speedbumps, will be worth the final goal.

By setting a roadmap in the lives of our young people through coaching, we can see how giving them appropriate age-level ownership of ministry leads to their having a sense of belonging in the family of God. They are then reassured they belong to God and their identities are in Him. Owning their faith through ministry engagement is crucial as they begin the process of identity formation, where passion begins to set a purpose in their lives. Further, learning to serve begins to develop a sense of compassion for those God calls us to serve. It is compassion that also gives us a sense of belonging. Compassion is rooted in empathy. When we experience struggles but are coached through them, we gain not only resilience but also compassion through empathy because we know what it is like to overcome a challenge. Practicing compassion helps others to belong. Once again, I can't think of any better words than to hear, "I have no greater joy than to hear that my children are walking in the truth" (3 John 1:4).

Questions

1. Why is it important to start teaching children this age how to set goals and to see those goals to completion?

2. Make a list of tasks you think your child is capable of doing at an age-appropriate level. For instance, doing their own laundry, helping with certain chores, etc.

3. Are there certain chores your child should get paid for and others they should do to contribute to the family?

4. Do you anticipate your children's mentors to change as they grow?

5. How do you begin to help your children capitalize on their strengths and abilities at this age *without* pushing him or her too hard?

6. How do you keep from living vicariously through your children and let them become the person God has created them to be? How can you coach without being critical?

7. How do words of affirmation let your child know they are loved for who they are, not what they do? How does pointing your child to Jesus, no matter what they do, help them know they belong to God and not to you?

Cultivating Years

"I Have Passion for God"

(Ages 12–24)

Chapter 5

Discipleship Model: Counselor

Leadership Theory

Transformational Leadership (Ages 12–18)

Erikson's Stage

Identity Versus Role Confusion

Biblical Example: Samaritan Woman

At this stage of life students begin the process of discovering what they are good at and what they enjoy doing (and what they do not like doing); thus, their understanding of interdependence comes with even more clarity. In this stage of life, we are moving away from the leadership roles of cop and coach to counselor, to begin a transformational process. The age group ranging from 12–18 years of age is known as "mid-adolescence." When your children are younger, you teach them the "rules of life." As they get older, you coach them on how to navigate through life using the rules they have been learning. At the mid-adolescence stage, you now cultivate within your children the ability to engage in the process of identity formation.

The theorist most responsible for transformation leadership theory is James MacGregor Burns, who proposed his theory in a book simply entitled *Leadership* (1978).[16] Similar to path-goal leadership, transformational leadership also taps into the motives of followers but does so in a way that helps the follower, the leader, and the organization. There are four components of transformational leadership: idealized influence, inspirational motivation, intellectual stimulation, and individualized consideration.[17] Leaders who engage in transformational leadership can be highly charismatic and have high moral standards. High moral standards are essential in the stage of life from ages 12–18 since these are the ages testing boundaries becomes somewhat normative. This is because teens are beginning the process of individuation—that is, discovering who they are apart from parent roles. This is especially true for older teens. Parents who display high moral standards are important to teens as they are moving into abstract thinking. Processing decisions becomes less black and white and can turn to grey. High moral standards are aspects of leadership shared with trait leadership. As you can see, some of these leadership models share similar aspects. Therefore, these leadership models can flow into one another while having nuances that help both the leader and follower. For individuals who seem to be demonstrating transformational leadership, yet lack high moral standards, they are practicing what is considered "pseudo-transformational leadership" or inauthentic leadership (Burns, 1978). These are folks who are pretty much leading for their own benefit. Once again, transformational leadership and discipleship share the common theme of engaging with the intent of being for the sake of others. Therefore, I reiterate that discipleship is leadership!

A significant strength of transformational leadership is that transformational leaders often provide a clear vision that is attractive, realistic, achievable, and believable. As we all know, early adolescents are prone to let their emotions get the better of them. Parents want to guide their teens into decisions that are realistic and believable. However, there is a tension between cultivating within our children "big dreams" without crushing their spirits. In my leadership, I have always taught, "We have a big God, so don't have small visions." What we must keep in mind with this statement is that it is God who makes achievements happen beyond our own abilities. We also must remember that our children will continue to grow by making competent decisions as they become adults. In the meantime, not only are you helping your children to cultivate a vision of their future, you are also cultivating a home that has secure attachments.

Transformational leaders are social architects that develop shared meanings, values, and norms. Hopefully, there have been elements of these traits as your children have been growing up in your home. Further, transformational leaders can be trusted even in uncertain and unreliable circumstances. In other words, as your children begin to explore the world outside the home, you are the architect of a stable home environment. Your home is where children come back to rest and find peace and stability. This sense of security at home allows your children to go boldly into the world knowing that they have a place to come back to that will restore their souls. Now, let's look at the four components of transformational leadership that were mentioned.

Idealized leadership is one in which the leader models the desired behavior to the followers. By modeling the expected behavior, the leader gains trust, respect and possibly admiration from the follower. This in turn motivates the follower to emulate the leader of those behaviors. In the case of discipling and leading your child, you are considering the dynamics of your home as you model discipleship as an integral part of your family and personal life. You may have heard the saying, "More is 'caught' than 'taught.'" By modeling a vibrant relationship with Jesus, you help your children learn how to reach their own spiritual and developmental goals. Once again, a common theme in many of these leadership roles is your modeling. As a part of modeling your relationship with Jesus, you are providing inspirational motivation as your life shows the value of being a part of something bigger than self. Your children will emulate the best of what you are modeling. When you set goals for yourself and your family, you can engage your child in setting and owning their own goals as well. As your child moves out of the concrete thinking stage of early adolescence, mid-adolescence is ripe for intellectual stimulation. Your children now become curious about other aspects of life outside the home, and they begin to gain a better understanding of how big the world is around them. Therefore, mission trips and serving opportunities for or with your children can help foster a sense of being involved in a world and life bigger than themselves.

Taking on the role of counselor becomes vital because you are helping your children process what they are learning about the world. Involved in counseling is the concept of individualized consideration—in other words, older teens start asking the question, "what should I do with my life?" These considerations are why high schools have counselors that help young people begin to discover what it is they want to do with their lives. Eighteen still seems too young for youth to know what they want to do with their lives, but helping to guide though this process is the role of a counselor—to guide youth through the process of individuation and self-determination. Individual considerations can include what a person has developed a passion for. Joining God in His Kingdom helps our children see they can have a passion for God and what He is doing in the world. Our children and grandchildren need to know they are at an age where they can make a difference. I truly believe you cannot discover your purpose until you discover your passion. So how does this process of self-discovery fit in with Erikson's model of psychosocial development? Perfectly, because Erikson identifies the key psychological conflict of identity versus role confusion for 12- to 18-year-old adolescents.

As children move from childhood into adolescence, they are learning how to become an adult. The term "adolescence" means to be in-between. In other words, adolescence is in-between childhood and adulthood. Adolescence is a natural movement toward individuation, that is, becoming their own individual. Adolescent youth are forming an identity that is their own apart from their parents' identities. They want to know what their place in the world is, where they belong, what they are passionate about, and who they are becoming. You may already begin to see the pattern. In early childhood, your child is looking for acceptance and belonging in the home. As they progress and get into older childhood, they are looking for acceptance and belonging in the community. In early adolescence, they are looking for acceptance and belonging among their peers. The process of moving into the world begins at the mid-adolescence stage, when your child is looking for acceptance and belonging in society. It is easy to see how these phases build upon each other.

As mentioned, the sad thing is that most parents begin to pull away from their mid-adolescent child thinking they need to "give their teenager space," but now is a time in life when our children need us most. Sure, they may "push away," but that does not mean they do not want us around. Remember, we represent our home, and our homes are safe places to fall back on. While there is some small truth to youth this age pulling away from their parents, too many parents pull out of their child's life too quickly at a time when identity formation is critical. It is normal for children to pull away. Remember, they are now trying to find their place in society, and what might feel like conflicts over values is simply young people trying to find their "place." It is at this critical time of their lives that your child needs to know they belong to God, and they also have a place of belonging with you.

The world offers too many conflicting worldviews that are contrary to what we are trying to teach our children. Parents give their children smartphones too early and take a dangerous risk of putting addictive pornography in a curious child's mind. Social media interactions can undo all the positive messages we have been trying to tell our children. I address these concerns in *Voices*, but suffice it to say, social media is a leading contributor to teen depression and anxiety. The constant barrage of messages from the world that tells our children who they should be is emotionally and spiritually overwhelming! So, instead of our children developing an identity as "God's child," their identity becomes soiled and distorted when they see themselves as addicted to pornography, getting their value from "likes" or "followers."

As we counsel our children to make wise decisions, we must remember to remind them of their identity and where they belong—even if a child seems to blatantly reject our values as parents. Children often model the faith of their parents and their peers. They have a conventional faith. The word *conventional* indicates a way of thinking that is similar to those who are around you in an affinity group. In other words, children learn their faith from their parents, then from their community, and even from their peers. Therefore, youth often come back from a youth retreat and seem "on fire for the Lord" only to have that fire dim within a matter of days or weeks. While conventional faith has its place, we want to move young people toward an integrative faith—that is, to a place where they own their own faith and make it theirs. No longer are young people parroting back the faith of their parents, but young people who have been discipled deeply begin to develop an integrative faith. My friend and colleague Dr. Robert Redman of South College points out that while James Fowler, author of *Stages of Faith* (1995), has some great principles of faith formation,[18] it seems that the role of the Holy Spirit is conspicuously missing.[19] In other words, while we may pursue discipleship by understanding social sciences, we must remember that it is the Holy Spirit who moves us (John 3:8).

A move toward integrative faith requires several processes to happen. First, a young person must be allowed to wrestle with difficult questions. Second, a young person must be free to explore faith as they see fit. Third, while a young person may be questioning doctrine or denominational teachings they have been taught by their parents or in their youth group, questioning is good because they are beginning to seek how to apply their faith to their real-life needs. If youth are shut down in their quest for deeper answers, then it is only natural they will seek answers elsewhere. Remember, at this age, young people are beginning to develop abstract thinking skills and can connect complex thought processes to deeper meanings. One of the recommendations I have in helping this process along is to let young people begin to teach in children's ministry—with guidance and training, of course! When they begin to teach, students discover information they may not have thought about in a deeper way because now they are responsible for teaching the material.

Biblical Example of Transformational Leadership

The Bible is full of transformational leadership examples. A great example is Jesus' encounter with the Samaritan woman at the well found in John 4:1–42. I encourage you to read this passage to be reminded of the nuances in this encounter. Jesus and the disciples could have done what every "good and orthodox Jew" would have done, which was to walk around Samaria. Sure, it would have added a significant amount of time to their journeys, but the Jews did not mingle with half-breed Samaritans (John 4:9). The Samaritans were considered unclean for many historical reasons—one of which was that they intermarried with their captors, the Assyrians. The Assyrians were particularly cruel people whom the Jews remembered from their captivity and oppression under the Assyrians. This is why Jonah did not want to go to Nineveh. It was not because he was afraid of the

Ninevites; rather Jonah knew that God was full of mercy and would redeem the hated enemies of Israel (Jonah 4:1–3).

Jesus broke with convention and went straight into Samaria. Of course, Jesus had a plan for this encounter, and like any good leader, the plan was for the benefit of the woman. Jesus initiated a conversation with the woman with a superficial question, "Will you give me a drink [of water]?" (John 4:7b). The conversation then morphed into a serious conversation when Jesus asked the woman to call her husband and come back (John 16). After a few more parlays, the conversation turned into spiritual revelations. Doug Fields, a well-respected and well-known youth ministry leader, offers this advice on how to engage in spiritual conversations with teens: every spiritual conversation can start with something superficial, move on to something serious, and then go deeper into the spiritual.[20] It is no wonder that Jesus used this approach as well.

As the conversation continued, the Samaritan woman opened up to Jesus and asked more questions. She was obviously spiritually hungry. There is an assumption in the text that the woman has been rejected by her own village due to her lifestyle. Frankly, her faith in humanity, and maybe her religion, had been on rocky ground. In that culture, having been with a total of six men, it is safe to assume that she had no positive identity of her own. Her conventional faith did not go deep enough. It is possible that she felt rejected not only by her people but also by God. Then Jesus showed up!

As she asked questions, there was no condemnation, there were no comments like, "Well, you should just pray more," or "You do not have enough faith," or "There is certainly unconfessed sin in your life." In fact, there was a good conversation of both the woman and Jesus hearing each other. An unmarried woman, a widow, or someone like the Samaritan woman had few—if any—prospects in that culture. They were often forced to compromise their moral values to survive. The experience this woman had with Jesus was certainly transformative. Not only was her life changed, it was *radically* changed. Let's consider the "four I's" of transformative leadership and how they came into play as the woman at the well interacted with Jesus. In reading the occurrence, the woman respected Jesus as she considered Him to be a prophet (John 4:19). Initially, she thought Jesus was just another Jewish man (John 4:9). Her mind is changed as she continues to dialogue with Jesus. John 4:28–30 shows how Jesus engaged in inspirational motivation as the woman began to tell her whole village that she believeed she had found the Messiah. We see that the woman was intellectually stimulated by the conversation in John 4:19–20. Idealized influence eventually led to the woman sharing her story with her entire village! (John 4:39–42). Finally, individualized consideration is engaged in when Jesus talked about the woman's life circumstances (John 4:16–18). The transformation comes about as she asked questions of Jesus and, most importantly, recognized that she was known by the Messiah! A woman who was once collecting water in solitude as an outcast then became a messenger of hope leading many others to believe (John 4:39).

Her life changed so drastically that she eagerly went into town to let the very people who had condemned her know that she found the Redeemer. Her questions did not drive her away from faith; instead, as she listened to the Master, her faith was not only restored but made magnificent. This woman, rejected by her own community, brought half of that community to a redeeming knowledge of Jesus Christ as Lord and Savior! The one who was cursed had become a blessing.

Redemption is a theme repeated with great frequency in the Bible regarding transformation.

This woman not only received wise counsel but also had her identity restored, and because she knew that she belonged to God, she rediscovered an identity she had lost—daughter of God! We then see what this woman did with her newly restored identity. She was filled with a passion to share the Good News that the Messiah had come! What a story! Stories of redemption, like that of the Samaritan woman, are the types of stories our young people need as their own. They need to know they will not be rejected for their mistakes. They will not be rejected because their need to ask questions is rooted in the deepest longing for answers in a fallen and hurting world!

The Bible is full of transformational leadership stories: Peter's reinstatement (John 21), Saul's conversion to Paul (Acts 22), the woman caught in adultery (John 8:1–11), David's moving from shepherd to king, God's moving Israel out of slavery to the Promised Land, and so many other occurrences in which people move from brokenness to transformation, healing, and redemption. The story of redeemed lives is the gospel story. In fact, stories of transformation happen as we practice many of the leadership models given as we engage in discipleship. The story of redemption moves us along the path of understanding that we are loved by God and that we belong to God. We are His redeemed children. We have worth as family members. Our lives are transformed, and this transformation compels us to share this story with all those around us, starting with our family members (Jerusalem) and moving to our neighbors (Judea), our community (Samaria), and, ultimately, to the world (Luke 24:47; Acts 1:8). If I can be so blunt, the Great Commission will not happen if we do not have a passion for God. We need to foster a passion for God and discipleship, and this process of leadership and discipleship must begin in our homes first. If it does not engage in the practice of discipleship, how do we expect to change the world?

Questions

1. How are you helping your child navigate toward identity formation? How can you help them develop a passion for God and for people?

2. Why is it difficult to move from the role of "cop" to "counselor"? What points of frustration do you experience? How can you work to overcome the frustrations?

3. What are some ways to begin moving from a coach to a counselor? What makes this transition difficult?

4. How does discipleship that moves through the various developmental ages and leadership models (to this point) help develop confidence and a sense of belonging in your child?

5. If you are struggling with this age, whom in your support group or church can you go to for advice without judgment?

Chapter 6

Discipleship Model: Confidante

Leadership Theory

Situational Leadership (Ages 18–24)

Erikson's Stage

Intimacy Versus Isolation

Biblical Examples: Paul, Nehemiah, and Ruth

The two main theorists behind situational leadership are Dr. Paul Hersey and Dr. Ken Blanchard. With situational leadership, there is an understanding that certain situations demand a certain type of leader, while other types of situations require another type of leader. As an example, one situation with a child might require you to be a servant leader, while another situation with another child might require you to be a transactional leader. Knowing how to respond to the needs of your children is another reason it is important to learn and practice a variety of leadership skills. I recently had a conversation with an individual who stated that he had always been a servant leader, and that servant leadership was the only model he had ever followed. Always being a servant leader sounds good in theory, but not in principle. What I mean is if you are always a servant leader and not a transformational leader when such a shift is required, there is a danger of fostering co-dependency between the follower and the leader.

In situational leadership, the leader adjusts the interaction he or she has to the needs of the followers. If a follower needs more direction, the leader offers the needed direction. If the follower needs less direction, the leader is more supportive. The approaches the leader can take when interacting with another are directing, supporting, delegating, or coaching. For instance, if the leader has a competent follower, the leader may decide to delegate since the follower needs little support or direction. The situation and the follower can determine the leader's approach. Another consideration is the follower's level of commitment. A follower with low motivation and low ability would be in the very lowest stages of development (Square S1—Telling), whereas a follower with high motivation and high ability would be in the developed category (Square S2—Delegating). (See diagram on page 79.)

There are four quadrants to consider for which style of leadership is engaged in. These considerations are based on the need for relationship behavior, which is supportive in nature, or for task behavior, which is directive in nature. A chart would reveal the following:

Leader Behavior

(*Supportive* Behavior)

Relationship Behavior

High Relationship **S3** Low Task Share ideas and facilitate in decision making **Participating**	High Task **S4** High Relationship Explain decisions and provide opportunity for clarification **Selling**
Low Relationship **S2** Low Task Turn over responsibility for decisions and implementation **Delegating**	High Task **S1** Low Relationship Provide specific instructions and clearly supervise performance **Telling**

(*Directive* Behavior)

Task Behavior

This diagram shows how your leadership style would flow through the various quadrants based upon the need of the follower. For instance, if you are teaching your 12-year-old how to mow the lawn for the first time, you may find yourself in square 1 because you may need to supervise with specific instructions so your child does not get hurt (directive behavior). However, if your child is 21 years old and has come to mow your lawn, you would be in square 2. If you are older and your child is 35 years old and has an injury, you may both discuss a plan, putting you in square 3. Square 4 would indicate a rationale for why you hired someone else to take care of your lawn. Either way, your leadership style is based on the situation. Situational leadership often relies on collaboration, information, and trust. Understanding this style of leadership fits well with Erikson's psychosocial development since the next stage is intimacy versus isolation.

McLeod (2018) notes the following about intimacy versus isolation:

> During this stage, we begin to share ourselves more intimately with others. ***We explore relationships leading toward longer-term commitments with someone other than a family member.*** Successful completion of this stage can result in happy relationships and a sense of commitment, safety, and care within a relationship. Avoiding intimacy, fearing commitment and relationships can lead to isolation, loneliness, and sometimes depression. Success in this stage will lead to the virtue of love [emphasis added].[21]

I offer a bit of pushback on the emboldened and italicized statement for this reason: if healthy relationships are navigated within the family unit, it is this healthy relationship that allows the 18- to 24-year-old to navigate loving relationships outside the home. Further, if healthy family bonding has happened during the first eighteen years of life, the relationship moves into a situational one in the sense that the young adult will go to his parents seeking help with adult issues.

For instance, in healthy family relationships, where might adult children go to if they need parenting advice? One would imagine their own parents. Based on the situation encountered by the young adult/adult (a lost love, a teething baby, a grandchild learning to drive, etc.), the parent (now grandparent) will be able to offer advice based on the situation and their experience. If a newlywed couple is facing challenges in their early marriage, they may find solace by seeking the advice of their parent(s); therefore, the parents become more of a confidante and give advice based on situations. In some ways, the parent may need to be more directive (for questions like "How do I file my taxes?"), and in other ways the parent may need to be more supportive (for issues like "I had an argument with my wife.").

When moving to the situational leadership role, it is important for parents to know the type of support needed for a certain behavior. By doing this, they become confidantes and help their children build confidence and competence. Good counsel and situational leadership can help young adults begin to discover what they are truly passionate about. Advice or counsel takes a lot of listening and evaluating the situation the young adult finds him- or herself in. It might be well and good to ask a child, "What do you want to be when you grow up?" However, a better conversation with young adult children is, "What are you passionate about?" Frankly, God has been a part of forming your child, as well as the situations that have been shaping them, since the day they were born.

Students frequently visit our college campus with their parents. These soon-to-be high school graduates are excited about the next chapter of their lives. Frequently, Christian parents—coming to a Christian college—will ask me, "Can my son make a living as a youth pastor?" I get it; parents are looking for their child to be able to eventually support themselves and a family, but these Christian parents are asking the wrong question (and they should know better). How many people have "good paying careers" but are miserable at their workplaces? I haven't had the guts to make the following comment when being face-to-face with parents, but I have wanted to ask, "Do you want your child to pursue a paycheck or their passion?" Here is the reward in following a God-given passion: if you love doing what you do, you not only will love going into work every day, but also will find ways to support yourself while doing what you love! I have spent every year, since age 18, doing youth ministry, and not once have I missed a meal. Yes, there are some months where I struggled, but I also learned to live within my means. Teaching financial principles can also be where parental and situational leadership comes into play. As parents, you do not (and should not, except in rare cases) bail your children out financially. Instead, the situation may require you to help your child develop a budget.

As our children build a relationship of trust with us, we move from being their parents to being adult friends. The move toward adult friendship is all based on trust, love, and intimacy in the sense that we know our children well. Let's be honest, if we are intentional about meeting the discipleship and psychosocial needs of our children, we will have a great rapport with them as they grow and mature. We will have the opportunity to cultivate a deeper relationship with them throughout their young adult years. Too many parents do this process backward. Too many parents have wanted to be their child's friend at a time when the child needed a cop or a coach. The imbalance in parent/child relationships is especially true when it comes to being a confidante. Parents who have come out of broken relationships have relied on their children to be confidantes and emotional support for them (Elkind, 1994).[22] God never intended for young children to become emotional support for their adult parents as a part of discipleship.

A biblical example of the difficulty in parenting at an older age can be found with Eli in 1 Samuel 2:12–26. According to one Jewish scholar and biblical records, Eli was at least 58 when Samuel went to live with him in the Temple. Nissan Mindel writes about Eli and his different relationship between his sons and his relationship with Samuel:

> Eli was a kind man by nature, and he was beloved by all the people who looked to him for spiritual guidance. Young Samuel was particularly attached to him, and faithfully followed his instructions. Eli was more proud of him than of his own two sons, Hophni and Phinehas, who, unfortunately did not follow in their father's footsteps. Taking advantage of their privileged position, they degraded the priesthood in the eyes of the masses by bribery and corruption. Eli rebuked his sons, but apparently not strongly enough. At any rate, they did not mend their ways.[23]

While this biblical example may be speculation, it is based on the information provided to us by Rabbi Mindel. The speculation is that Eli may have been a little too kind with his children when his children needed a more solid hand at discipline. Further, Eli probably served as more of a grandparent-mentor role to Samuel, and thus the deeper relationship between the two. What is certain is that Samuel had a different heart than Hophni and Phinehas. As someone who has adopted three sons, the youngest being adopted when I was approximately 43, I can speak from first-hand knowledge that I did not have the energy I needed when he was 11 years old.

I have learned that situational leadership is valuable because all three of my sons learned differently, and each of them had different personalities, traits, character, trauma, and many other aspects that formed them to be who they are. I am thankful that God's Holy Spirit has intervened on countless situations. I will say as a single-parent and someone who is getting up in age: single-parenting and "re-parenting" at a grandparent age are not ideal situations. The growing number of non-traditional families, who are believers, is all the more reason we need a supportive community and intergenerational mentoring!

Biblical Example of Situational Leadership

I cannot begin to think of a better example of someone who practiced situational leadership than the apostle Paul. (Of course, Jesus does exemplify all these leadership models, but I don't want to give the "Sunday School" answer of "Jesus.") Paul was a "Pharisee among Pharisees" (Acts 23:6) and also a Roman citizen (Acts 16:37). Who could have been better to take the good news of Jesus as Messiah according to Jewish prophecies to the Gentiles? Paul needed the understanding of how to take a Jewish Messiah to the Gentile people and to understand Gentile thinking and culture. Further, Paul needed to display situational leadership when it came to meeting the individual needs of each of the churches God had him plant. The church in Ephesus was different from the church in Corinth. Even more so, Paul had to use situational leadership in helping young Timothy pastor a church.

When it comes to passion, Paul was clearly a passionate person (Acts 22:3). While Paul was a passionate person, God had to do a dramatic work to change Paul's purpose from being one who persecuted the Church and Christ (Acts 9:4) to a person who boldly proclaimed the gospel. Further, Paul stated that he became whatever he reasonably needed to become to all people so he might win them to Christ (1 Corinthians 9:19–23). We also see through his epistles that Paul was a great motivator of others and mastered both relationships and tasks while also releasing others, like Timothy, for ministry. The situation in Paul's life dramatically changed, so much that Paul was willing to go from being the one who killed Christians or put them in prison to being the one who was put in prison and ultimately martyred for his faith. I have often told folks, "Until you discover what it is you are willing to die for, you have never really lived!"

Nehemiah

Nehemiah is another great example of situational leadership. Nehemiah was the cupbearer for King Artaxerxes (Nehemiah 2:1). Nehemiah was completely crushed by the fact that Jerusalem was in ruins. To rebuild the wall around Jerusalem, he had to constantly adapt to threats and challenges as he was building the wall. Nehemiah recognized the threats that came against the plans to rebuild the wall, but, manifesting a deeper awareness, Nehemiah recognized where the threats were coming from. Look at Nehemiah 4:7, "But when Sanballat, Tobiah, the Arabs, the Ammonites and the people of Ashdod heard that the repairs to Jerusalem's walls had gone ahead and that the gaps were being closed, they were very angry." What you might notice is that all of the people listed, who were going against Nehemiah and the Jewish people, belonged to ethnicities who had a history of being enemies of Israel. Nehemiah had to adapt plans because of the threats of enemies. Depending upon the situation, Nehemiah was a diplomat (Nehemiah 2:1–5) or a warrior (Nehemiah 4:16–23).

What Nehemiah and Paul both have in common, besides situational leadership, is that they were both passionate and knew their life purposes. Their passion contributed to their purposes. These are the seeds we need to be planting into the hearts of our young people as soon as possible. When we begin to see a passion in our children's lives, we need to nurture those passions so our children begin to walk down the path of discovering their purposes in life.

Ruth

Ruth is another great example of someone who displayed marvelous situational leadership. Ruth showed an unbelievable passion and love for her mother-in-law, Naomi. Even though Ruth could have gone back to be with her people, she refused to leave Naomi all alone to fend for herself. Ruth was someone who took a great deal of initiative to care for Naomi (Ruth 2:1) as she went out to glean wheat from the field of Boaz, and Boaz showed incredible kindness to Ruth. As their relationship grew, Ruth found in Boaz both a kind man and a "kinsman redeemer." The developing relationship between Ruth and Boaz was, of course, all of God's orchestrating, yet Ruth was wise enough to understand situational leadership as she cared for Naomi and took advantage of what God had provided. Further, Ruth listened to Naomi's advice and showed great humility in how she approached Boaz. A long story made short, Boaz and Ruth were married, and Ruth became part of the lineage of Jesus. Ruth becoming part of the lineage of Jesus was all because Ruth followed God with a heart of compassion and knew how to read a situation.

Good situational leadership is just that: leaders evaluating the situation and making wise decisions that benefit all involved. As the biblical examples illustrate, situational leadership can cultivate within the leader and the follower a passion to follow God and to do what is right.

Questions

1. Why is it so difficult of a process to start "letting go" of our children?

2. What are some of your concerns as your children enter this stage of life? Are some of your concerns unfounded?

3. Throughout your child's life, you have had to learn how to surrender them to God. How do you surrender your teens to God at this stage of life?

4. If you reflect on your child's progress in life, what do you wish you would have been more intentional about when it comes to discipleship?

5. Has a local church been instrumental in your pursuit of discipleship for your child? Why or why not?

6. How can you begin to give wisdom to other parents who are now going through stages you have already been through?

7. How do you keep from "owning" your child's concerns or problems while still being supportive?

Cultivating Years

"I Have Purpose in God"

(Ages 25+)

Chapter 7

Discipleship Model: Companion

Leadership Theory

Authentic Leadership (Ages 25+)

Erikson's Stage

Generativity Versus Stagnation   Biblical Example: Josiah

Remember that the various leadership models will often build upon or overlap one another. Think of situational leadership. Sometimes, you will need to change your leadership style based upon what your child and your family are facing. Personally, I argue that the first foundation of leadership begins when a child is born, and aspects of servant leadership are practiced throughout a child's life. Beginning with servant leadership as a discipleship model certainly goes against the current issue of the systemic abandonment of our young. If servant leadership is the bookend at the beginning of childhood, I personally believe that authentic leadership is the opposite bookend at adolescence. While the intent of this book is not to thoroughly discuss the current debate on whether "young adults" are in a period called "emerging adult" or "extended adolescence," both periods of time are occurring simultaneously. Adolescence begins with the biological markers of puberty and ends with social markers. (I would add that adolescence ends with social markers and biology since the pre-frontal cortex is not fully matured until age 24. Maturation is why your emotionally healthy adult child will come back and admit that you were much smarter than he thought you were when he was a teen.)

Young people who are preparing for their futures and taking responsibility for themselves are entering the "emerging adult" stage while adolescents who are not engaging in responsible and mature decision making are still in the "extended adolescence" stage. For others, who reach typical "adult age" but have not matured, the term of "kidult" has been suggested. Kidults are adults who act more like kids due to their seeming inability to mature. When a young person becomes an addict, the maturation process is interrupted, which offers an explanation for why addicts who are adults in their bodies but are still in adolescence in the way they process information. If a young person becomes an addict at age 14, this is usually the age where their cognitive development becomes "stunted." It takes years of sobriety to allow the brain to play "catch up" and mature. The ability to still be able to mature throughout life is the good news of neuroplasticity. While I did not want to digress, I felt it important to mention why there may be delays in young adult development.

In 2003, Bill George presented his leadership theory in *Authentic Leadership: Rediscovering the Secrets to Creating Lasting Value*. Authentic leadership is exactly what it sounds like. A leader is perceived as authentic or "real" to the followers. Authentic leadership is a newer leadership theory initially postulated out of transformational leadership by Bill George of Harvard (2003)[24] who built upon the works of Bass (1990),[25] Bass & Avolio (1993),[26] Bass & Steidlmeier (1999),[27] Burns (1978),[28] Howell & Avolio (1993),[29] and (Northouse, 2019).[30] One of the difficulties in clearly defining the authentic leadership model is due to the complex process of having no single definition of authentic leadership (Northouse, 2019). Authentic leadership is interpersonal and developmental, meaning this leadership style places a heavy emphasis on relationships. The theory also assumes that all leaders can grow in their incorporation of authentic leadership practices. Key marks of authentic leadership are transparency, self-awareness, internalized morality, and balanced processing. Authentic leadership also has a high degree of affective, relational, and passionate drives. Leaders who are self-aware, have high moral standards, are driven by causes bigger than themselves, and, in the right environments, can be great motivators for followers of causes. Much of the internal affective and empathetic characteristics of an authentic leader are shaped by the leader's critical life event experiences (Northouse, 2019). It will be easy to see how this leadership model fits well into Erikson's stage of generativity versus stagnation.

Some strengths of authentic leadership are that it elicits trust and confidence among followers. Second, the approaches to implementing authentic leadership are broad and non-limiting. A third strength of authentic leadership is that it has a strong moral dimension where the leader is driven to do what is morally right. Finally, there are some instruments, such as the authentic leader questionnaire, that have validated authentic leadership as a proven leadership model.

A weakness is that there are concerns as to how a leader's values relate to the leader's self-awareness. In other words, a leader might think he or she is practicing authentic leadership, but the values do not match the behaviors. More research needs to be conducted on whether positive psychological capacities make authentic leadership too broad of a concept. Further, what is not certain is how Millennials or Gen Zers will function under an "authentic" leader. Finally, more research needs to be done on the validity of authentic leadership having a measurable impact on goals and outcomes.

Authentic leaders often share the attribute of a willingness to lay down their lives for a larger cause. Nelson Mandela certainly displayed authentic leadership—especially during his trying circumstances of being imprisoned during South African apartheid. Others who have displayed authentic leadership have been Mahatma Ghandi, Martin Luther King, Jr., and, of course, Jesus. Some leaders know how to exhibit multiple leadership styles. Certainly, Jesus knew how to exhibit the right leadership style at the right moments. Further, many of the disciples were authentic leaders since they were willing to lay their lives down for a cause bigger than themselves.

I hope my children grow into mature adults that not only long for an authentic relationship with me but, more importantly, long for an authentic relationship with God. It is my prayer that my children move from a "conventional" faith into an "integrative" faith where they no longer adopt my faith; rather they have a vibrant faith of their own. Notice all the values listed in the Authentic Action Wheel[31] that are also necessary for discipleship to occur.

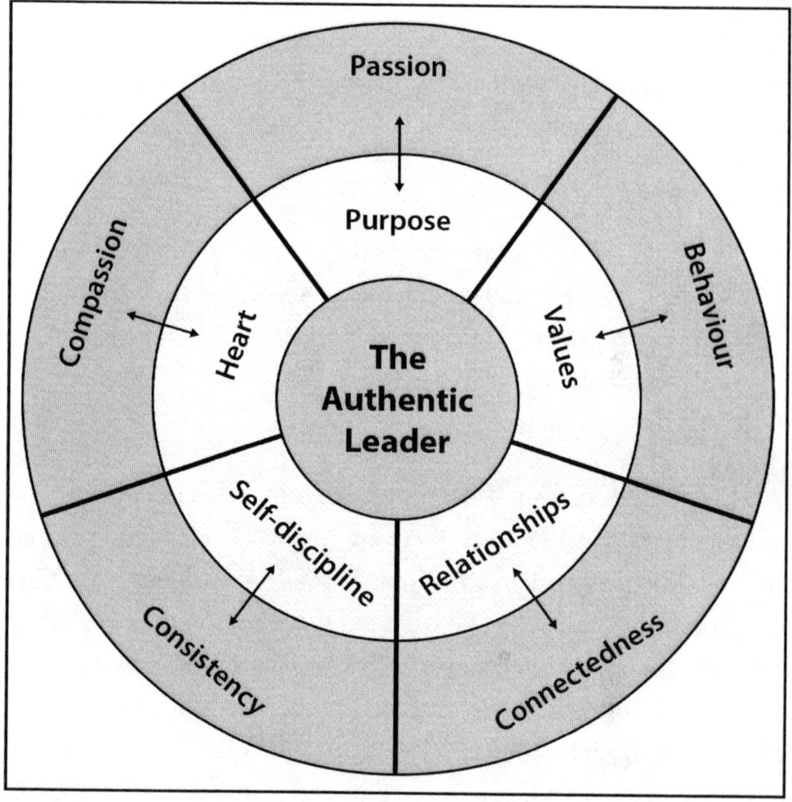

Source: George, B. (2003).

It is easy to see why authentic leadership can only come from a person who has reached higher degrees of maturity. Authentic leadership now becomes a leadership style that you display to your adult children as they become companions with you through life. Think about it this way: you and your child have lived a lot of life experiences together. You have moved through stages of serving (Matthew 2:28), correcting and rebuking (2 Timothy 3:16–17), developing character (1 Corinthians 15:33), coaching (Ephesians 6:4), counseling (Proverbs 15:22), and confiding (Proverbs 11:13), so it seems appropriate that adults who have built their relationships on these foundations would become companions in life as found in Psalm 55:12–14. Let's take a look at these verses:

> If an enemy were insulting me, I could endure it; if a foe were rising against me, I could hide. But it is you, a man like myself, my companion, my close friend, with whom I once enjoyed sweet fellowship at the house of God, as we walked about among the worshipers.

These verses convey a deep and meaningful relationship with others and with God. Further, there are implications for companions who are close and passionate about life and about being with God and other worshipers. If we go back to our definition of discipleship, we can see that these three verses above imply believers who have not walked away from each other or their faith. As a reminder, here is that definition of discipleship: "Disciple-making is the process by which the Holy Spirit works through the inspired Word, related materials, and Spirit-empowered workers to 1) lead individuals to Christ, 2) build them up in Christ, and 3) equip them for effective, lifelong ministry for Christ" (Parker, 1999, 19).[32] When we do discipleship well, we help our children accomplish the primary task of adolescence: identity formation. Engaging in a solid discipleship approach will also help our children learn how to become their authentic selves.

The verses above give a sense of deep abiding passion for life while also giving purpose in life. I should also state that discipleship shares a common theme with the definition of spiritual formation: "Spiritual formation is the process of being formed in the image of Christ for the sake of others" (Mulholland, 16).[33] When we know who we are, we know our purpose and we are more inclined to serve others because our identity is rock solid in Jesus Christ! These are the kinds of attributes that I want to see in the children I raise!

Now, as our journey in this book moves out of adolescence into adulthood, I will focus on Erikson's stage of generativity versus stagnation,[34] a stage usually reserved for those who are 40 years of age and older. Yes, young adults are primarily in the stage of intimacy versus isolation, but I truly believe that if young people have been discipled well and know they are loved while also knowing how to love others well, it is easier to transition into generativity. A person who is secure in their identity is more likely to engage in healthy intimacy rather than to struggle with isolation. Those who are secure in their identity may also be ready to impact the world around them because of the confidence they obtain through healthy relationships. While young or old may need more skill development, they can see their lives as lives that matter and can make a difference in the lives of others. I know that classically trained psychologists would want to push back against my statements but let us remember that the Holy Spirit can certainly work through younger people as well. Let's look at this stage of generativity versus stagnation, and you can determine for yourself if there is any merit to my statements.

Psychologically, generativity refers to "making your mark" on the world through creating or nurturing things that will outlast an individual. Middle-aged individuals experience a need to create or nurture things that will outlast them, often having mentees or creating positive changes that will benefit other people. This may also circumvent the "mid-life crisis" based on questions of a person's purpose and identity.

Biblical Example of Authentic Leadership

Even though Josiah began his reign at a very young age, it is clear to see that all the elements of the authentic action wheel are a part of Josiah's character. At just age 26, Josiah was clearly a young king who had a sense of passion and purpose when it came to restoring the Temple of the Lord. He trusted other leaders who were responsible for various aspects of the work on the Temple (2 Kings 22:7) and his kingdom (verse 9). As the Temple was being repaired, the workers found the Book of the Law. When Josiah heard the Book of the Law being read aloud, he tore his robe in a sign of repentance. He clearly wanted what was in the best interest of the Israelites (verse 13). Due to his humility and seeking after God, God promised Josiah that reign and ended his life in peace.

Josiah displayed many of the attributes found in the authentic action wheel, and because of his authenticity, the people of Judah were spared from immediate calamity. In chapter 23, we see that Josiah called the people together to hear the Word of God with the expectation that they would all live accordingly.

Josiah lived a life that was full of instituting change and making a difference. He spent his whole life clearing out all the pagan practices Judah had found itself involved in. You can see a bit of this account in Exodus 23:20–26. We are even told that the angel of the Lord would go before the people of Israel, and they were to obey the angel.

Josiah was basically doing what the Israelites had failed to do. Upon hearing the word of the Lord through the Law, Josiah had no choice but to wipe out all these places of idolatry. Josiah had to cleanse the land because of how evil Judah had become. It seems that Josiah's singular purpose had become that of restoring Judah's relationship with God. In some sense, the desire of every Christian parent is to know they have lived a life where their children and grandchildren have become "lifelong disciples involved in effective ministry for Christ." A natural overflow of walking with Jesus is the desire to reproduce Christians within, and outside, our family. By engaging in discipleship and engagement, we join Christ in His Kingdom work and enlarge His family.

One final word about Josiah that should bring hope to all of us parents who have "prodigal children." Josiah's father was named Amon. Second Kings 21:20–22 says,

> He did evil in the eyes of the Lord, as his father Manasseh had done. He followed completely the ways of his father, worshiping the idols his father had worshiped, and bowing down to them. He forsook the Lord, the God of his ancestors, and did not walk in obedience to him.

Even though Amon was evil, God intervened, and Josiah did the opposite of his evil father and grandfather. For those of us who try our best to do what is right in discipling our children, I believe God will honor that. If God can redeem Josiah from an evil immediate family member, how much more can He redeem our wayward children when we have strived to raise them to know God?

Questions

1. In many ways, when we look at the authentic action wheel, these are the characteristics we want our children to have while living a godly life. What advice would you now give other parents who are still going through the earlier stages and ages? What have you learned?

2. How do you foresee becoming a confidante to your children in a way that is life-giving?

3. Considering Josiah's heart for God and his family background, how does Josiah's story offer you hope for your children?

4. At the end of your life, what would you want your children to say about you as a parent?

5. What words of advice would you give your children, or others with children, in regard to discipleship and leadership as a parent?

6. How do you plan to build a legacy of discipleship in the lives of your children and grandchildren?

Chapter 8

Concluding Thoughts

There are certainly other models of leadership one could consider engaging in when discipling children and youth. The irony is that we are in a period of time when there is a plethora of material available that offers ways to disciple our children, and yet we continue to increasingly grow as a biblically illiterate society. The lack of biblical literacy—especially in our own homes—illustrates there is a lack of intentional pursuit when it comes to discipling our children. Yes, discipleship is leadership, but it is also a battle for the hearts, minds, and souls of our children. Ephesians 6 begins with what was considered "the household" or "the family" in Paul's day. It is no wonder that the next section begins the discussion about spiritual warfare and identifying the enemy. I cannot help but think that we have relegated this Scripture to the childhood portrayal of the armor of God. Without an intentional means of discipling our children, we are sending our children into a real battle with plastic toy shields and weapons—and then we wonder why depression and anxiety are such a strong spiritual factor in our children's lives.

In fact, at the time of this writing, gun-related deaths among adolescents have surpassed automobile accidents. Automobile deaths among adolescents have decreased while firearm deaths have increased (Goldstick, et. al., 2022).[35] While there are no definitive reasons for the increase in firearm deaths, we might consider that the research was conducted in 2020. As we know, COVID-19 significantly impacted the nation's mental health. Our young people are struggling with increased mental health issues as they were removed from their normal socializing environments. We might conclude that automobile deaths decreased due to less driving among teens while firearm related violence increased due to isolation. One thing that is certain; COVID-related or not, our young people are facing an unprecedented perception of loneliness through what Dr. Chap Clark (2011)[36] would call "systemic abandonment" and what Mark DeVries (2004)[37] would call "systemic isolation." COVID-19 only accentuated that loneliness and made it more apparent. Let's read a little of what my friend Mark DeVries writes about the consequences of systemic isolation:

> Teenagers today are in trouble. And what they don't know can literally kill them. We are sending them into adulthood ill prepared for the increasing demands of our complex society. Like so many children in the Middle East who defend themselves only by throwing rocks at soldiers with machine guns, this generation of teenagers enters the confusing battleground

> of adulthood armed with nothing more than vague values and innocuous religious experiences.
>
> As in any war, there are casualties. Teenagers are dying at a higher rate than they were forty years ago—victims of accidents, suicide, homicide, drugs, and alcohol. While the members of every other age group are more likely to live than they were forty years ago, adolescence has become for many a life-and-death obstacle course (DeVries, 2004, 35).[38]

These indicting statements are now twenty years old. The writings of Dr. Clark, Mark DeVries, and many others remind me of the warnings child psychologist Dr. David Elkind started writing about in *The Hurried Child* (1981).[39] Subsequent books by Dr. Elkind, *Ties That Stress: The New Family Imbalance* (1994)[40] and *All Grown Up and No Place to Go* (1998),[41] give the picture of being like one "calling in the wilderness" (Isaiah 40:3; Matthew 3:3; Mark 1:3; Luke 3:4; and John 1:23). The problem is that in this wilderness, there are few who seem to be listening to the desperate voices of young people and those of us who work with them. It is as if all the red flags and warning signs have been ignored by our society.

The time to step up as Christian parents and disciple our children has never been more urgent! From the time a child is in the womb until death parts the parent and child relationship, a parent's voice is the most important voice that can point children to God. Combatting loneliness, isolation, and anxiety is part of what makes a parent's voice the most important voice a child can hear. As a reminder, we as parents represent the voice of God, so we must get discipleship and leadership right. In our current culture, we may feel like the voice in the wilderness as well, but we cannot dismiss the value of our voice!

We cannot sit idly by expecting someone else to disciple and lead our children. If I can be so bold, even as a trained youth worker who has been working in student ministry for decades, my voice will *never* hold the value of your voice—and it shouldn't! If my voice and leadership are louder than your voice and leadership, there is a significant disconnect between you and your child. This scenario is far worse if the voice and leadership of the world are louder than yours.

If you do not know where to start, no matter the age of your child, start somewhere! Start a group of like-minded parents who imagine what discipleship can look like. The struggle is worth it. Also, remember that there is an ebb and flow between life stages and leadership models as presented. Nothing is etched in stone, but you must rely on the Holy Spirit to guide you. This book challenges parents, grandparents, and people who care about children and youth to start the discipleship journey somewhere. No one is expected to be perfect, but everyone is expected to grow emotionally and spiritually. Emotional and spiritual growth are markers of maturity. If you expect maturity and discipleship of your children, you should be engaged in the discipleship process yourself. Remember, discipleship and leadership do not have to be "professional." In fact, one of the primary reasons parents stop discipling their children is because there is an expectation that "there is someone better equipped than me can do this." No one else lives with your child day in and day out and no one (other than God) knows your children better than you do! Yes, go to a local church for guidance, support, materials, curriculum, or whatever you need—but go! Don't do discipleship and leadership by yourself. Remember Jethro's advice to Moses! Stop doing it all by yourself but don't put the full responsibility on others. These are wise words to follow!

As with engaging in attachment therapy, parents can go back to previous stages of development and leadership theories as needed by observing what is going on in their child's life. These ways of leading and discipling cascade down into each other. We should never lose the desire to be like Christ to our children. You may need to adjust, go back, and cover areas that need strengthening. Navigating between the stages of psychosocial development and discipleship stages your child is going through is understandable. In fact, reviewing lessons learned may be required. Maybe you are a parent who is new in a relationship with Christ. You can always "go back" and grow with your children. Maybe you are a parent who has been walking with the Lord for many years, but you realized you have "dropped the ball" when it comes to a discipleship approach and to leading your children. That is okay too. Your kids may resist you at first, but in the long run, they will respect you for trying and not giving up! The stakes are too high not to try something!

I have always told my volunteer leaders that youth ministry is a seed-planting endeavor. The same is true of being a parent, grandparent, teacher, or youth worker when it comes to discipleship. There is a reason that Jesus talks about the seed (the gospel) and the soil (the heart) (Matthew 13:1–23). It is easier to plant a seed than it is to nurture it. Nurturing takes a much longer time, and yet the better the soil and the better the nurture, the better the produce. Leadership guru John Kotter reminds us that 80% of change does not come from information; it comes from the heart (2012).[42]

I had to learn one lesson the hard way as a parent. The better the parent you are, the more inadequate you can feel. The feeling of inadequacy is referred to as "imposter syndrome." Imposter syndrome is a psychological distress with a fear of being discovered as a fraud and can cause inadequate performance during times of transition (LaDonna, 2018).[43] Imposter syndrome can keep us from setting and achieving goals because we fear being inadequate. Since our children are transitioning from one stage and age to another, it can feel overwhelming to try to figure out how to be the best parent *now.* Parenting is certainly a "learn as you go" enterprise but trusting in God's Word and the leading of His Holy Spirit and collaborating with other parents can help overcome imposter syndrome! Parenting can feel like going to the grocery store: once you finally figure out where everything is, the managers at the store move the product you are looking for. You feel as if you are just getting to master one stage of life, and before you know it, the next stage is happening. Now add more than one child who thinks and acts differently. It is no wonder life can feel overwhelming, but I encourage you to keep working at discipleship and leadership. It will all be worth it—eventually. If you are simply actively listening to your child, asking what they think about the Bible, having conversations about God, and walking through life together, you are not an imposter. You are a parent.

One other reminder: if you think about it, Adam and Eve had the perfect Parent (nurture). They were in the perfect environment (nature). God would walk and talk with Adam in the cool of the day in the garden. They had everything they could ever want. God had given them passion, purpose, and a plan, and yet Adam and Eve still rebelled. There are no guarantees as a parent, but we can "stack the odds." We can disciple and lead our children. We can take them to church and seek out mentors for them—even when they do not feel like it. When your kids rebel, remember, it is not the seed they are rejecting; it is just the soil that needs tending. As the parent, you have the right—and the responsibility—to know who your child's friends are. You even have the right to meet their parents. While you may be the most significant influence in your child's spiritual life, you cannot ignore the evil one who snatches the seed, the rocky soil, or the thorns. You are the parent. Trust the Holy Spirit and do not dismiss the "gut checks" that you have.

Partner with like-minded people who share your vision for discipleship. Get a group together and work together. Work *with* your pastor, youth pastor, children's pastor, or whoever it is in your church who can help get you resources. On the same note, do not be afraid to recommend resources to your church staff and other parents. If there is a family, children's, youth, or parent ministry event coming up, take advantage of it. Go to a D6 Conference. The investment will be well worth it! Most of all, make discipleship fun for both you and your child. While engaging in fun activities and having conversations, be sure to look for "God moments" or teachable moments that can point the hearts of our children to Jesus! We can talk too much about Jesus only if we are being inauthentic about Him.

By putting this book into practice, you now have a place to begin engaging, discipling, and leading your children (and maybe their friends) in their walk with Jesus. Engaging in these practices will become the most rewarding experience in your life! Share your stories of struggles and how God broke through due to your efforts in partnering with Him. Your stories will encourage other parents, grandparents, teachers, and youth workers! Move forward in His peace, love, and guidance, and may these blessings flow to your children. Be fruitful and multiply!

Summary Chart

Age	Psychosocial Development	Leadership Model	Biblical Example	Message	Parent Role
Birth–1.5	Trust Vs. Mistrust	Servant Leadership	Jesus/Paul	I am loved by God	Christ
1.5–3	Autonomy Vs. Shame/Doubt	Trait Leadership/ Learning Skills	David the shepherd	I am loved by God	Character
3–6	Initiative Vs. Guilt	Transactional Leadership	David/ Nathan	I belong to God	Cop
6–12	Industry Vs. Inferiority	Path-Goal Leadership	Moses/ Jethro	I belong to God	Coach
12–18	Indentity Vs. Role Confusion	Transformational Leadership	Samaritan Woman	I have passion for God	Counselor
18–24	Intimacy Vs. Isolation	Situational Leadership	Paul, Nehemiah, Ruth	I have passion for God	Confidante

Endnotes

Introduction

[1] Parker, M. (1999). *Making healthy disciples.* The Christian and Missionary Alliance.

[2] Erikson, E. (1950). *Childhood and society.* W.W. Norton & Company.

Chapter 1 – Servant Leadership (Ages Birth–1.5)

[3] Parris, D. L., & Peachey, J. W. (2013). A Systematic Literature Review of Servant Leadership Theory in Organizational Contexts. *Journal of Business Ethics, 113*(3), 377–393.

[4] Howell, Don. (2003). *Servants of the servant: A biblical theology of leadership.* Wipf & Stock Publishers.

[5] Wilkes, Gene C. (1998). *Jesus on leadership.* Tyndale House Publishers.

[6] Spears, L. C. (2009). Servant Leadership. *Leadership Excellence, 26*(5), 20.

[7] Staff. (2022). Attachment-Based Therapy. *Psychology Today. https://www.psychologytoday.com/us/therapy-types/attachment-based-therapy* (Accessed January 21, 2023).

[8] Van der Watt, J. (2017). The meaning of Jesus washing the feet of his disciples (John 13). *Neotestamentica, 51*(1), 25–39.

Chapter 2 – Trait & Skills Leadership (Ages 1.5–3)

[9] Stogdill, R. M. (1948). Personal factors associated with leadership: A survey of the literature. *Journal of Psychology, 25,* 35–71, and (1974). *Handbook of leadership: A survey of theory and research.* Free Press.

[10] Katz, R. L. (1974). Skills of an effective administrator. *Harvard Business Review, 64*(2), 178.

[11] Mumford, M. D., Zaccaro, S. J., Connelly, M. S., & and Marks, M. A. (2000). Leadership skills: Conclusions and future directions. *The Leadership Quarterly, 11*(1), 155–170.

Chapter 3 – Transactional Leadership (Ages 3–6)

[12] Los Angeles Police Department. (n.d.). LAPD motto. https://www.lapdonline.org/lapd-motto. (Accessed January 26, 2023).

[13] Juneja, P. (2008). Transactional leadership theory. *Management Studies Guide. https://managementstudyguide.com/transactional-leadership.htm* (Accessed January 23, 2023).

Chapter 4 – Path-Goal Leadership (Ages 6–12)

[14] House, R. J. (1996). Path-goal theory of leadership: Lessons, legacy, and a reformulated theory. *The Leadership Quarterly, 7*(3), 323–352.

[15] Erikson, E. (1950). *Childhood and society.* W.W. Norton & Company.

Chapter 5 – Transformational Leadership (Ages 12–18)

[16] Burns, J. M. (1978). *Leadership.* Harper & Row.

[17] Afshari, L. (2022), Idealized influence and commitment: A granular approach in understanding leadership, *Personnel Review*, Vol. 51 No. 2, 805–822. https://doi.org/10.1108/PR-03-2020-0153 (Accessed January 26, 2023).

[18] Fowler, J. (1995). *Stages of faith development: The psychology of human development and the quest for meaning.* Harper One.

[19] Redman, R. (January 9, 2023) Doctor of Ministry, Youth and Family Ministry seminar lecture. South College Online.

[20] Fields, D., & Robbins, Duffy. (2007) *Speaking to teenagers.* Youth Specialties Academic.

Chapter 6 – Situational Leadership (Ages 18–24)

[21] McLeod, S. A. (2018, May 03). *Erik Erikson's stages of psychosocial development. Simply Psychology.* www.simplypsychology.org/Erik-Erikson.html. (Accessed January 23, 2023).

[22] Elkind, D. (1994). *Ties that stress: The new family imbalance.* Harvard University Press.

[23] Mindel, N. (2011). *Eli the high priest.* Kehot Publications Society. https://www.chabad.org/ library/article_cdo/aid/112391/jewish/Eli-The-High-Priest.htm (Accessed January 27, 2023).

Chapter 7 – Authentic Leadership (Ages 25+)

[24] George, B. (2003) *Authentic leadership: Rediscovering the secrets to creating lasting value.* Jossey-Bass.

[25] Bass, B. M. (1990). From transactional to transformational leadership: Learning to share the vision. *Organizational Dynamics, 18*(3), 19–31.

[26] Bass, B. M., & Avolio, B. J. (1993). Transformational Leadership And Organizational Culture. *Public Administration Quarterly, 17*(1), 112.

[27] Bass, B. M., & Steidlmeier, P. (1991). Ethics, character, and authentic transformational leadership behavior. *The Leadership Quarterly, 10*(2), 181–217.

[28] Burns, J. M. (1978). *Leadership.* Harper & Row.

[29] Howell, J. M., & Avolio, B. J. (1993). Transformational leadership, transactional leadership, locus of control and support for innovation: Key predictors of consolidated-business-unit performance. *Journal of Applied Psychology, 78*(6), 891.

[30] Northouse, P. (2019). *Leadership: Theory and practice* 8th ed. SAGE Publications.

[31] George, B. (2003). Authentic action wheel. *Authentic leadership: Rediscovering the secrets to creating lasting value.* Jossey-Bass.

[32] Parker, M. (1999). *Making healthy disciples.* The Christian and Missionary Alliance.

[33] Mulholland, M. Robert. (1993) *Invitation to a Journey.* InterVarsity Press.

Chapter 8 – Concluding Thoughts

[34] Erikson, E. (1950). *Childhood and society.* W.W. Norton & Company.

[35] Goldstick, J. E., Cunningham, R., & Carter, P. (2022). Current Causes of Death in Children and Adolescents in the United States. *The New England Journal of Medicine.* 386 (20) 1955–1956. https://www.nejm.org/doi/full/10.1056/nejmc2201761#article_citing_articles (Accessed January 31, 2023).

[36] Clark, C. (2011). *Hurt 2.0: Inside the world of today's teenagers.* Baker Academic.

[37] DeVries, M. (2004). *Family-based youth ministry.* IVP Books.

[38] Ibid., 35.

[39] Elkind, D. (2001). *The hurried child: Growing up too fast too soon.* Da Capo Press.

[40] Elkind, D (1994). *Ties that stress: The new family imbalance.* Harvard University Press.

[41] Elkind, D. (1998). *All grown up and no place to go: Teenagers in crisis.* Perseus Books.

[42] Kotter, J. (2012). *The heart of change: Real-life stories of how people change their organizations.* Harvard Business Press.

[43] LaDonna, K. A., Ginsburg, S., & Watling, C. Rising to the level of your incompetence: What physicians' self-assessment of their performance reveals about the imposter syndrome in medicine. *Academy of Medicine* 2018; 93 (5):763–8.